Music and Musical Instruments of the Garo Tribe of North-East India

Music and Musical Instruments of the Garo Tribe of North-East India

IRIS WATRE THOMAS

AKANSHA PUBLISHING HOUSE
New Delhi - 110 002 (INDIA)

AKANSHA PUBLISHING HOUSE
4649-B/21, Ansari Road
Darya Ganj, New Delhi - 110 002
Ph.: 23263193/9811582579
Fax: 011-23263193
Email: ektabooks@yahoo.com

Music and Musical Instruments of the Garo Tribe

First Published 2007
ISBN 81-8370-079-9

PRINTED IN INDIA

Published by M.P. Misra for Akansha Publishing House, New Delhi and Printed at Aryan Enterprises, Delhi

CONTENTS

FOREWORD

This is a path-breaking research work in the sense that even till today, there is hardly any work done on this line of investigation and more so, in the case of the Garos of north-east India.

That the Garos are music lovers and enjoy their lives to the full to the beating of musical instruments have been testified by all writers, foreign, Indian and local. Starting from John Elliot, the Commissioner of Dacca, the first European ever to visit the Garo Hills during 1788-'89 till the visit of Prof. Robbins Burling of Michigan University, USA in 1997, all the accounts given by them referred to them as lovers of music and merry–making. Similarly, many of the Indian writers such as T.C. Sinha, B.N.Choudhury etc. also testified to this fact. The local writers such as D.S. Rongmuthu, not only confirmed this finding but has dealt with some of these Traditional Songs and Musical Instruments in his works.

However, none of them has dealt exclusively on this aspect of Garo cultural life. Some of them, at the most had extracts of their songs and descriptions of their musical instruments in their works. Even the local literary figure, Shri D.S.Rongmuthu, had dealt with only an epic song in his "Epic Lore of the Garos" and included the Garo music and musical instruments as part of his works on Garo culture in some other books. As such, the Garos do not have any work as yet fully devoted to this aspect of Garo life and culture.

This book entitled "Music and Musical Instruments of the Garo Tribe of Northeast India" is substantially based on finding of her. M.Phil. dissertation, has come out as the first of its kind, and the author herself being a member of the community and being adept in music and musical instruments could handle the subject with confidence and authority which added to the beauty of the book.

I am quite sure that the book will be well received and appreciated by all who come across with it.

(M.S.Sangma)
Former Pro-Vice-Chancellor
N.E.H.U., Tura Campus

PREFACE

Extensive studies have been made on the sophisticated music and musical instruments of India, but till date, no one has shown serious inclination towards the music of the North-East. In my humble way, I have tried to record what I have seen of the instruments, and what I have heard of the music, of the Garos of Meghalaya. The Garos are a simple, happy carefree people who express every little mood through music, which has become their way of celebrating life itself - the happy moments as well as the sad. I believe they have much to contribute to the world of music.

During my research, I had received the support and help from many people starting with my husband Eugene, my children Shane, Adrian and Gail, parents, other family members, friends and well-wishers. I thank them all for their patient support, inspiration and encouragement.

I am immensely indebted to Prof. Milton S. Sangma, former Pro Vice-Chancellor of North-Eastern Hill University, for his invaluable guidance, advice and encouragement without which this work would not have materialised.

I am extremely grateful to Mr Llewellyn R. Marak, late Mr Mihir N. Sangma and Dr. Julius L.R. Marak for the encouragement that they gave me by making valuable documents available to me and for the suggestions they offered.

I thank all respondents who had spared their time for the interview with me, and who had demonstrated the method of playing the various traditional musical instruments.

I acknowledge with thanks all the assistance given by the staff and officials of the Eco-development Society of Meghalaya, Tura who had helped me reach the interior areas of Garo Hills.

I am specially indebted to The Rev. Presley B. Lyngdoh, Mrs. Pauline Warjri and late Dr. Orester J. Kharpuri who performed the difficult task of writing the staff notation for the songs.

I hope, I am not wrong in believing that my experience and labour will be useful to those who read this book. I shall welcome suggestions on correction or other improvements to be considered in future revisions of this work.

IRIS WATRE THOMAS

1

LAND AND THE PEOPLE

Garo Hills, the land of the Garos or *A.chiks* (as they prefer to be called today, *A.chik* meaning hill man), lies to the South-west of Assam, 25°9' and 26°1' North latitude and between 89°49' and 91° of East longitude. It was formed into a district in 1866 and is now part of the state of Meghalaya. It is bounded by the districts of Goalpara of Assam on the North and West; Khasi Hills on the East and the Mymensing district of Bangladesh on the South. In 1867 Tura was established as the permanent headquarters of the district by the then British government of India. Today, the Garo hills has been subdivided into three districts, namely—East Garo Hills, West Garo Hills and South Garo Hills.

The Garos are a section of the Great Bodo family which traces its origin to the Tibeto-Burman race of the Tibeto-Chinese family of North-West China. The area that lies between the upper waters of the Yang-tse-kiang and the Ho-wang-ho. Folk tales speak about their settlement in a country known as Mandalae.[1] Invasion from a ferocious Northern tribe is said to have brought about their subsequent migration

1 Dewansingh S., Rongmuthu, *Folktales of the Garos*, Dept. of Publication, University of Gauhati, 1960, p. 345. Mandalea - probably the name of an ancient Garo country in Upper Burma. It may also mean the ancient Garo village which developed into the modern region of Mandalay in Myanmar.

to the North-West, beyond the "*Arurongdi*" river, which is probably the Irrawady river in Myanmar. As a result a large contingent of *A.chiks* settled in "*A.song Tibotgiri*", the ancient Garo name for the country of Tibet. In course of time, the land in *Tibotgiri* on which the *A.chiks* had settled down became drier and drier. The cultivated soil yielded little return and gradually changed into arid waste. This led to the second stage of migration further west towards *Garwar Bri*[2] which probably refers to the Garhwal hills in the Himalayas. Thence they proceeded to the country south of the hills and reached the Assam valley which was like a "land of milk and honey" after the arid landscapes they had passed so far. The reason for their migration are clearly given in the extracts of a song which runs thus:

A.ba cha.na a.namja,
Mina dango minamja,
Kilgron puo kilojana,
Songdongna a.song gitalko am.na
Chiringna chiga dingdangko nina.[3]

Which says that

As the fields are arid,
Rice crops are poor,
Cotton seeds do not germinate,
To search for new land
And look for fresh flowing streams and rivers.

"*A.song Nenggitchu Chiga Nengchibing*", identified as Nokcholbari,[4] became the first *A.chik* settlement in the region of *Kalibong* in Bhutan, also known as Dhon Kuta. Their second settlement was at "*A.song Patari Chiga Suunchi*" claimed to be Cooch Behar.[5] Their third settlement was

---

2 *Ibid.*, pp.1-2.

3 Jobang D. Marak, *The Garo History*, Part I & II, West Garo Hills, Meghalaya, 1982 (2nd ed.), p.2.

4 Dewansingh S. Rongmuthu, *op. cit.*, p. 341.

5 *Ibid.*, p. 341.

"*Udare Jakbri Mehgongma Kolatchi*" which is the ancient Garo name for Rangamati.[6] Their fourth settlement was in "*Chiga Binengbineng*" in Habraghat. During their migration from Tibet, the Garos of old brought along with them not only the language, culture, beliefs and tales of their original home, but also a distinct love of music. They even carried along with them some musical instruments which they felt impelled to carry, like the various types of *Rangs* or gongs; *Kakwas* or cymbals; *Gaanti* or bells; *Susuaks* or anklet bells; *Singas* or trumpets. This can be deduced from the words of the following traditional song

Rajiko skang chilate,
Do.pako jaman chakate,
Jappako, Jalingpako, Nokmako Saneko mikkango done,
Janggil meroriko ra.bite,
Ki.me matjangchiko jakkipe,
Kakwa doke, silcha chime
Gaanti morokroke,susuak mojokjokke,
Gitchi bajing ole, Konkona ra.e,
A.song Patariona, chiga suunchiona,
Behar Rajani songo dongnapeaha.[7]

The English translation of this song says that they came –

Led by *Raji* (Warrior) and followed by *Dopa* (Warrior) in the rear,
Jappa and *Jalingpa* placing Sane (*Nokma*- Chieftain) in the front,
Carrying the life-giving rice grains on their backs,
Clasping the Yak's tail, Clashing their cymbals and shields,
Clanging of bells and the jingle of the anklet bells,
With spades and picks
They reached Cooch Behar
And sojourned in the land of the king of Cooch Behar.

They finally crossed the Brahmaputra river on rafts of banana stalks and settled in the nearest hills on the southern bank. Later on, strong differences of interest and opinion

---

6 *Ibid.*, p. 342.

7 Jobang Marak, *op. cit.*, p. 3.

surfaced and they broke up. Some remained at the base of the hills, while the majority made for the jungle[8] and came to occupy the dense hills of the present Garo hills. The Garos entered the hills in batches from different directions and settled in different sections, which resulted in the evolution of certain linguistic and cultural variations amongst them. As a result, they are divided into thirteen groups, viz. the *Am.bengs*; the *A.kawes* or *Awes*; the *Chisaks*; the *Duals*; the *Matchis*; the *Matabengs*; the *Matchi Duals*; the *Chiboks*; the *Rugas*; the *Garas*; the *Ganchings*; the *Atongs* and the *Megams*.

The Northern section of the mountain area is inhabited by the *Awes* or *A.kawes* which is adjacent to the districts of Kamrup and Goalpara. They are mainly cultivators as is evident from their name, *A.kawes* which means "ploughers of the plain."

The *Chisak* group occupies the North-Eastern part of the Garo hills, and lives in the region bordering the Awes. They inhabit the eastern bank of the *Simsang* river (Sameswari).[9] The word "*Chi*" means water and "*sak*" means above. Therefore, *Chisak* refers to the Garos living in the area above the water source,[10] renowned for their skill in bamboo products as well as food preparation of delicacies from bambooshoot.

The *Duals* occupy the area directly south of the *Chisaks* on the banks of the river *Simsang*. They have the reputation of being excellent fishermen, and specialise in preparing dry fish.[11] A great number of this sub-tribe dwell in the Mymensing district of Bangladesh.

---

8 Gabrielle Bertrand, *The Secret Lands Where Women Reign*, London, Robert Hale Limited, 1958, p.44.

9 Julius L.R. Marak, *Garo Customary Laws and Practices*, Vendrame Missiological Institute, Shillong, 1985, p.3

10 Milton S. Sangma, *History and Culture of the Garos*, Books Today, Oriental Publishers, New Delhi, 1981, p.135.

11 Gabrielle Betrand, *op. cit.*, p.45.

The heartland of the Garo hills is occupied by the *Matchis* and they are famous for the production of cotton.

The *Matabengs* or the *Matjangchis*, who are more or less a mingling of *Am.bengs* and *Matchis*, are found towards the north of the *Simsang* river, in between the *Am.bengs* and *Matchis*.

The *Am.bengs* inhabiting the western section, constitute the largest division of the tribes. They populate nearly half the area of the district including Tura. Like the *Matchis*, they are also known for their cotton cultivation.

To the East of the *Am.bengs* we find the *Chiboks*. They live in the upper *Bugi* river valley, upto the *Dareng* river.

The *Gara-ganchings* occupy the southern areas extending from the *Nitai* river nearly to the Sameswari river. They have a distinctive craftsmanship in wood sculpture and ingenious technique in house construction.

The *Atongs* occupy the *Simsang* valley and the hills in its vicinity as far as *Siju*.[12]

The *Me.gams* inhabit the area bordering West Khasi hills.[13] They seem to be a fusion of the Garo and Khasi tribes. In appearance and custom they closely resemble the Garos, but have their own dialect which cannot be understood by the Garos. Dr. Grierson has classified them as Khasi.

A great number of Garos can be found in the neighbouring states like Assam and the Mymensing district of Bangladesh. They retain their various divisions, language and custom, but have acquired some of the nature and ways of the majority people among whom they reside.

Social Organisation

The Garos are divided into various "*Chatchis*" or clans. The most notable clan being the *Maraks, Sangmas* and *Momins*. The other clans are the *Shiras* and *Arengs*. These

12 Milton S. Sangma, *op. cit.*, p.134.

13 Julius L.R. Marak, *op. cit.*, p.3.

clans are again sub-divided into numerous sub-clans or "*Ma.chongs*" which claim descent from a common motherhood.

The whole Garo Hills is divided into many clearly defined areas known as "*A.kings*". Each *A.king* is under the ownership of a particular *ma.chong* such as *Nengminja, Rangsa, Gabil, Ampang, Chambugong*, and so on. Each of these *A.kings* are placed under the guardianship of a custodian-cum-supervisor known as the *Nokma (A.king Nokma),* who is selected by the *ma.chong.*

Marriage

The marriage customs and laws of the Garos are based on the matrilineal system, according to which the descent is always traced from the mother. Marriage is governed by two important laws namely, exogamy and *A.kim*, which means that a man and a woman intending marriage must belong to different motherhood. Thus a *Nengminja Sangma* cannot marry another *Nengminja Sangma*; a *Watre Momin* another *Watre Momin*; *Rangsa Marak* another *Rangsa Marak* etc. Those who violate these customary laws commit what is known as *Madong* and *Asimalja.*[14] Rules of *Madong* were violated in a marriage between a *Koksi* and *Koksi; Bakdong* where a union takes place between a *Koksi Sangma* and a *Nengminja Sangma*; and *Asimalja* would literally mean something forbidden, taboo, not done, having strong moral connotation. These are considered incestuous and serious crimes punishable by death.

The young boys and girls seldom got an opportunity to meet each other, so they made the most of the various festivals and ceremonies that take place throughout the year, like the *Wangala, Ganna* mite and *Mangona* ceremonies. The market place also, besides being a centre for trade, serves as an ideal place for socializing. Here the young girls get the chance of meeting and choosing their life

---

14 *Ibid.*, p.97.

partners. For, in the traditional Garo custom, marriage proposals must always come from the girl's side. Even in modern times, though the choice is made between the two individuals, a formal proposal has to come from the girl's side. The girl does not personally propose to the boy, but indicates her choice to the male members of her family who make the necessary negotiations and arrangements. An interesting and exciting feature here is the capturing of the boy, who is caught unawares, any where at any time and brought to the girl's house. According to Garo etiquette, it is customary for the boy to resist this marriage at least twice although he may be quite willing to marry the girl. However, if the boy manages to escape the third time, it is taken for granted that he really does not wish to marry the girl, and he is allowed to go free.[15]

Besides the legal form of marriage, the Garos have about ten types of marriage which cannot be regarded as legal or formal, but are all the same recognised by customary laws and are prevalent among the *songsareks* (pagans). These are *Cha.senga* (staying in lover's house); *Nokkromna sala* (taken to be the husband of the heiress); *Nape tua* (entering and sleeping); *Chame jika* (baiting for life partner); *Dokchapa* or *on.chapa* (providing an additional wife); *Jikgite ra.a* (second wife); *Seke kima* (marriage by elopement); *Nokpante gaa* (to climb the bachelors dormitory); *Cha.dila* (to induce to eat); *Chawari rima* (to capture a son-in-law). The formal ceremony that is performed to legalise these marriages is the *Dosia* ceremony (*Dosia* - killing a fowl).

Divorce

The matrimonial bonds among the Garos, however, are very loose, but adultery is very severely punished by the tearing of the ear lobes and garments in the case of a woman in olden days. The man found guilty of adultery was either

---

15 A. Playfair, *The Garos*, London, David Nutt, 1909, p.67.

sold in slavery or killed.[16] The customary law of the Garos permits a man and a woman to seek divorce on certain grounds and must be initiated and approved by the woman's *chra*, i.e., the male members of the family. The *chra* consists of the maternal uncles, great uncles, nephews and brothers of the same *ma.chong* (motherhood). Divorce may be sought on the following grounds:

1) When a wife or a husband commits adultery (*somal donna*)
2) When a man or woman is insane.
3) When a wife and husband cannot live together anymore and desire separation by mutual consent.
4) For being hermaphrodite or when either party proves sterile.
5) When a husband or wife is cruel and is a cause of fear or harm and injury in the mind of the other partner *(Bamgija wachagrika)*.
6) When a wife or husband denies conjugal union.[17]

The cause of the separation is inquired into by the village elders and the actual divorce accomplished by the '*Bol seki den.a*' ceremony (*Bol* - tree, *den.a* - cut). However, now-a-days it is more common for the injured party to seek redress in the civil court, or to apply to a *Laskar* (local magistrate) for compensation as well as dissolution of marriage.[18]

Inheritance

Being a matrilineal society which claims descent from the motherhood, the system of inheritance is also influenced by this. There exists a definite account about the decision taken in respect to the question of inheritance, as given by Jobang D. Marak. According to the narration, the *A.chik*

---

16 *Ibid.*, p.97.

17 Julius L.R.Marak, *op. cit.*, p.125.

18 A.Playfair, *op. cit.*, p.71.

and the *Dikgil* patriarchs assembled together in *Matia Panchia* of *Me.gam Amejang*, in the house of Bonepa. It was the sons of *Siram* who first broached the question, as to who should be the inheritor - the sons or the daughters? To this, the children of Noman suggested that it should go to the '*demechik*', i.e. the daughter, and *Ruga Kotchu* seconded this view. It was the *Doli* people who suggested that the householder should bring in the nephew as the son-in-law, a view which was endorsed by Muga Dingsepa and Raja Sirampa. Ever since, this has been the customary law followed by the Garos in regard to inheritance. All property belongs to the woman and is passed on from mother to daughter. In case there is no female issue, a daughter of the elder or younger sister is chosen as the next heir. In case such an heiress is unavailable, then the nearest female of the clan is approved by the clan members as the inheritor. The property is thereby retained in the motherhood. Men do not inherit property, for if the sons are allowed to lay claim on the properties of the mother, these would pass out of her *machong* or clan, which is never allowed.[19] Men, however, can acquire (purchase) land of their own. This will, however, pass on to the wife according to the usual law of inheritance and this in turn goes to the daughter - thus reverting to the motherhood.[20]

Economic Life

As far as the economy of the Garos is concerned, it is greatly dependent on agriculture. Cultivation is their main livelihood and means of subsistence in which the whole family takes part. Trade is carried out on the seasonal products of the land such as, paddy, millet, cotton, ginger, betelnut, fruits and vegetables like oranges, banana, maize, job's tears (*Coix Lachyrma-Jobi*), chillies, melons, yam, sweet potato, and pumpkins.[21] In the old days brisk trade was also done in a limited amount in indigo and lac.[22]

---

19 B. Choudhury, *Culture and Linguistic Aspect of the Garos*, Lawyer's Book Stall, Gauhati, 1958, p.38.

20 Julius L.R. Marak, *op. cit.*, p.141.

21 A.Playfair, *op.cit.*, p.45.

22 *Ibid.*,p.46.

The Garos practise shifting cultivation which is known as Jhum cultivation. They follow a calendar laid down by Bonepa Janepa the first person to perform all the rites connected with jhum cultivation, as instructed by *Misi Apilpa Saljong Galapa* to *A.ni Apilpa chini Galapa*, another patriarch who was the first among the humans to obtain rice seeds. Bonepa, as the first jhum cultivator in the hills of *A.chik a.song*, invented the names of the jhum months as follows[23]:

1.	*Gamalkaja*	- March	7.	*Mejaphang*	- September
2.	*Mebakja*	- April	8.	*Ahnija*	- October
3.	*Jagro*	- May	9.	*Berokja*	- November
4.	*Sohgalja*	- June	10.	*Kilokja*	- December
5.	*Jagapja*	- July	11.	*Awitja*	- January
6.	*Jamebok*	- August	12.	*Wachengja*	- February

The hills are divided into hundreds of *a.kings* (clan territory) which were under the Clan Chief. The headman of the village called *A.king Nokma* distributes the lands of jhumming equitably amongst the families living in the village under him. Each family starts the clearing of the jungle in their own plots between the months of December and February. All the capable members of the family work in the jhum fields[24] known as '*A.ba.*' The land is used for two consecutive years before being abandoned for six or eight years. In the first year, all the crops are planted together, but during the second, the land is devoted exclusively to rice. Since a new patch is opened each year, two fields are always simultaneously under cultivation. One plot is planted with mixed crops and the other with rice alone. Weather and other factors permitting, all crops should be available for harvest each year.[25]

---

23 Dewansingh S.Rongmuthu, *op.cit.*, p.289.

24 B.Choudhury, *op.cit.*, pp.21 & 22.

25 Robbins Burling, *Rengsanggri*, University of Pennsylvania Press, 1963, p.27.

Nokpante or Bachelors' Dormitory

A unique feature of the Garo society is the importance given to the proper training and grooming of the young men of the villages through the institution of the *Nokpante*. *'Nok'* means house and *'pante'* means bachelor. Such houses existed in every *A.chik* village, each clan having its own *nokpante* for their own youths.

When the boys reach adolescence they are sent to sleep in the *nokpante* at night as the Garos regard it improper for a grown up boy to sleep with his parents and sister in the same house. Besides serving as a common dormitory, it has other important purposes too. It was essential that every young man learns all kinds of skills and handicrafts before entering married life. Thus, it was here that the Garo youth was given training in the various skills of art, craft, music, carving and painting with indigenous colours extracted from natural sources like roots, leaves, barks, etc., making of baskets, fishing nets, musical instruments as well as the art of playing these instruments, making of hunting and war implements, the art of warfare, defense as well as training in discipline and physical fitness. Agricultural know-how was also imparted, which was considered a must for every young man, as it was the main source of livelihood. It was the skilled elders of the village who took the responsibility of imparting their skill and knowledge to the younger generation, and thereby keep alive the old traditions and culture. Every young man was expected to keep himself physically fit and to be vigilant for the safety of the village. Life in the *Nokpante*, in fact, was an education in the art of living[26] where the youth learns discipline and are moulded into men with all round skill, personality and sense of responsibility.

Various folk songs, mythological folklore, traditional accounts, ancient tales of war and adventure, principles of animistic worship, etiquette and morality were also taught and narrated by the elders and *the Katta agangipa* (Folktale narrator).

---

26 JuliusL.R.Marak, *op.cit.*, p.161.

The other uses of the *Nokpante* was as an assembly place for the village elders and young men,[27] whose opinions were also considered as important in decision making. It also served as a court room of the *Nokma* or the *Laskars.*[28] At times the *nokpante* even became a guest house for strangers in the village.

The structure of the *nokpante* is distinctly different from the dwelling homes. It is much larger in size and stronger too, as it is built with solid timber posts of *Sal* or some other strong wood. It is also the most decorated and adorned building, as every pillar and post is etched with beautiful carvings of animals, birds, lizards and people, done on one solid block of wood, by the young men themselves. Even the steps leading to the *nokpante* is a whole tree on which steps have been carved out.

An interesting and unique feature of the *nokpantes* in the villages of *Siju* and *Emangre* is the intricately carved and coloured king-posts called '*Do.kaku*' by the people, which resembles the totem poles of the American Indians. As to the origin of this art narrated to me by Aldat Sangma of *Siju* village, he said that it was *Siju me.apa Aseng Dimseng Sangma* and *Emangre pante Sutik Dentik mamasa* who first constructed a *nokpante* at the instruction of the spirit *Katchi a.ning Do.pagisim* (spirit king Crow of the underworld). He taught *Rongkan,* another man, the technique of carving a *Do.kaku* out of the *Gamare* wood and colouring it with seven different colours red, blue, dark green, parrot green, black, yellow and white, which could be obtained from natural sources. Red was obtained from the bark of a tree which is first dried and then boiled to obtain the colour and yellow from the root of *the "mese nachil"* (wild bougainvillea). Green was obtained from three sources, (a) *nirri* leaves, (b) *chengrang* leaves and the root of the *Alot Matchadu.* Blue was obtained

---

27 *Ibid.*, p.163.

28 Sinha, Tarunchandra, *The Psyche of the Garos*, Calcutta, 1966, p.93

from the *chalue* leaves, black from the bark of the *Dokime* tree and white from a soft white material which is available between layers of rocks. Once water is mixed and dried, this material becomes as hard as a brick.[29] The *do.kaku* was meant to give an attractive touch to the *nokpante*, to lure the female folk. The *Do.kaku* is also supposed to be bestowed with the mystic power of protecting man from misfortune. As the legend goes, a youth by the name of *Chengot* was being chased by a man-eating tiger. Finding no place to hide, he quickly took shelter in the *Nokpante* by climbing right up to the king-post and hid behind it. The bright colours of the *Do.kaku* blinded the tiger and prevented it from seeing the youth. In this way *Chengot* was saved from a horrible death.

Women were strictly forbidden to enter the *nokpante*. If by accident a maid even climbs up two steps, she was to give a fine of one pig and a jar of rice-beer, and a cleansing ceremony commences to remove the defilation. However, girls were allowed to enter the *nokpante* on special occasions like *chugan ringa* or post-funeral ceremony, *Galmak doa* or *Amua*, i.e. festivals after the burning of the jhum fields and during the time of the construction of the barns (*mi jam*).[30]

Agricultural Festivals and Ceremonies

Agriculture being their occupation, their main festivals and ceremonies coincide with the various stages of cultivation throughout the annual agricultural cycle. They attach much importance to the worship of the spirits which rule the seasons, to maintain harmony with the spirits and thus obtain their blessings in the form of good harvest. They start their festivals with due solemnity, through invocations and prayers made to various spirits of the jhum season. These ceremonies slowly build up towards the final

---

29 As told to me by Agat Sangma of Siju village.

30 Julius L.R. Marak, *op. cit.*, p.158.

and most important social function of the Garos, the "*Wangala*" or harvest festival, during which a lot of feasting, singing, dancing and other social activities take place. An important feature is the *Katta Agana* or story telling by the bards and minstrels, and singing competitions through the singing of *Doroa* and *Ajea* where competitors try to out-do each other. It is a time for romancing for the young and the choosing of life partners.

The annual festival begins with several preliminary religious ceremonies which commence from the beginning of the year. The first of these is the *Opata* ceremony,[31] when a man first decides on the plot of land which he intends to cultivate. If he has a good dream that night he takes it as a good omen and starts cultivating. However, if he has an unpleasant dream then he takes it as a bad omen and abandons the plot and looks for a better one.

The next ceremony is the *Den Bilsia* ceremony also known as *Gitchipong roka* or *Asiroka*. This marks the cutting down of the trees and bamboo and the clearing of the land, and takes place in the month of January and February. Here the ritual of '*Okamdoa rimdosola*'[32] (inviting and bringing up) is performed in the *Nokma*'s (clan chief's) house, for *Rokimema* the goddess of rice, pleading her to dwell in their field and thus bless it with good harvest. The Garos believe that if the land is not cleared of all uncleanness and disease, *Minimaa Rokime* (mother of rice) will not bless them with her presence. So, they not only clear their jhum fields at this time, but also their homes and surrounding areas.

The *A.galmaka* or *A.gal doa* ceremony follows this. According to Robbins Burling, it "is second only to *wangala* in importance". This is the jhum burning ceremony of the new field and the first of the important rituals in connection with the jhum cultivation festival. Here a cock and rice

---

31 A. Playfair, *op. cit.*, p.93.

32 Mihir N. Sangma, *Maniani Bidik*, Garo Hills Book Emporium, Tura, 1989, p.5.

beer is offered (*Churarona*) to invoke the blessing of *Sre-Tonggitchak-Warika*,[33] the mother of the god of fire, to free the land from any profanation, pollution, and desecration through fire. In front of the *Kimdim* or *Sambasia* (sacrificial alter) which is made of bamboo, offerings of fowl, fish, and cooked rice is also made to *Rokime*, for her blessings on their jhum fields. Then millet seeds are scattered in all directions for good harvest. After the sowing of the seeds everyone returns to the village. The elders circulate from house to house in the day time and the young visit the same houses at night. Time is generally spent in feasting, dancing, and merry-making.

The next important festival is *Rongchu gala* or *Ginde gala*[34] which is a thanksgiving for the first fruits to *Misi Saljong*, the God who first taught man the technique of cultivation. It is said that previously, the Garos lived only on the natural and seasonal products of the land, like a variety of yam and herbs. It was *Misi Saljong* who gave the first rice seeds (*mi bitchri*) the seeds of which were handed down from generation to generation as *Rongjanggi* (life giving seed) and taught the technique of cultivation - using the seasons. Thus, the rainy season indicated the time of sowing the seeds and the dry season marked the harvest period. The offering consists of freshly plucked and pounded, flattened or powdered rice or millet, served on a plantain leaf. The other items offered are citrus fruits and sugarcane cut into pieces and sprinkled with rice beer. There is great feasting and singing and playing of gongs but no dancing takes place. Following this a small but special ceremony is observed called *Jamegappa-Ahaua*[35] which signifies the reaping of the jhum products. While carrying the last sheaves of crop to the house, the children follow the person carrying the sheave and utter the sound "*Ahaua*". The rice grains of

33 Julius L.R.Marak, *op. cit.*, p.64.

34 Milton S. Sangma, *op. cit.*, p.239.

35 Julius L.R.Marak, *op. cit.*, p.68.

the *Medong* or sheave are kept to be made into the rice beer to be used during the *wangala* festival.

Finally, we come to the most important festival and that is the *Wangala* or harvest festival, which ushers in the final stage of cultivation. It is believed that it was the God of the underground *Meenma Drongma*[36] who enlightened man on the details of performing the *wangala*. This is celebrated with great pomp and grandeur and gay abandon, when the harvest of all jhum crops have been fully gathered, in the month of October. The day for celebration is fixed according to the convenience of each village and goes on for a week. The Garos will not take any of the crops produced in their jhum lands till the performance of the *wangala*. There is a deep underlined meaning behind the observance of this festival. It is a moment of thanks-giving to *Misi A.pilpa Saljong Gatapa* (gods), as well as a bidding of reverent farewell to the Gods who have blessed them for the year. The *wangala* celebration can be divided into two stages. The first stage *Chu-Rugala*[37] is a solemn ritual performed by the priest (*Kamal*). The rice beer prepared from the "*Medong*" (rice specially set aside for rice beer), and no other beer is used during this ceremony as offerings to *Saljong*. *Chachat* or incense are burnt at the centre post of the house. Following this rice powder is mixed with water into a paste with which the posts and beams of the *Nokma*'s house is decorated. This is done in every house. The guests are also smeared with this paste on their backs. This is known as *Wanti toka*.

The second stage is *Chachat soa*[38] meaning burning of incense. The Garos get their incense (which is a form of resin) from the bark of a certain tree called *Chachat bol*, which they believe was made by God before all other trees. This ceremony is performed by the priest in the *Nokma*'s house, where the sacred drum is hung. On this day, rice is

36 Mihir N. Sangma, *op. cit.*, p.13.

37 R. Burling, *op. cit.*, p.64.

38 *Ibid.*

scattered all around the *Nokma*'s house signifying the season of rain and hail. Incense is burnt till the whole room is smoky to signify the coming of rain clouds. Throughout this ritual the *kram* or sacred drum, the Rang or gong and the *Dama* or big drums are played ceaselessly. When the ritual is over, rice and curry is served directly by hand to all the guests amidst much joviality. The young and old form their own groups and start dancing to the beating of drums, gongs, blowing of flutes and horns, led by the *Nokma* who does the "*Grika*" or warrior dance. The dancers present about fifty different styles of dancing imitating animals and birds and depicting everyday events. This is also the time for choosing of life partners. Folks sit around the fire and sing songs related to *wangala* like *Ajea, Dani doka, Kurama sala, Ohomai, Kore doka, Doro agana, gosai ringa,* etc. The culminating ceremony is the *Rusrota*[39] ceremony observed for the safe keeping of the crops in the granaries.

Another festival celebrated by the *A.kawes* and *Chisaks* of the North and North-Eastern region is *Gure Wata*[40] or releasing of the horse God, who is taken as the God of fertility and wealth. This stems from the belief that, if due reverence is not given to this deity it can take away the fertility of the land on which one is cultivating. It is most probable that the importance of the horse comes from the respect given to the '*Matchik*', the Garo name for Yak, which was brought along with them from the land of Tibet when they first migrated. Being an agricultural based society, the fortunes of a man depends greatly on the soil. The image of a horse is fashioned out of straw and plantain trunk, decorated and taken round the whole village by the priest, followed by dancing villagers. This goes on for three days and two nights. Finally, the horse is taken to a stream and thrown into the water. The head, however, is preserved for the next year.

---

39 A. Playfair, *op. cit.*, p.95.

40 *Ibid.*, p.94.

The customs and traditions and other cultural traits of the Garos narrated above, are only few aspects of some of the vast and varied Garo culture. However, most of these traditional-cultural patterns have been giving way, in course of time, to various outside influences.

2

MUSIC AND CLASSIFICATION OF SONGS

Music is an art form in which sound is organised in patterns that please the listener. It can be created by one person singing to himself or herself, or a large group singing in chorus. It can exist purely for its own sake, or can be closely involved with other activities, particularly with religious ceremonies, and with dance which is 'musical movement'. The basis of traditional music is 'Melody' - the tune, and the pattern of different 'notes' give melody an up and down shape, like the contours of a landscape. These patterns formed by different lengths of notes give melody its 'rhythm' or shape in time.[1] The combination of musical instruments also adds colour to music. Rhythm, melody and harmony are thus the basic elements of music. The art of music is universal, as it knows no linguistic and social division. It originated in the past from the spirit of joy and delight. It finds its way of expression in the human world as a result of its creative urge and stimulus. It has a living and driving force that makes men dynamic in the field of activity.[2]

1 *Modern Century Illustrated Encyclopedia*, Vol.14, McGraw-Hill Far Eastern Publishers Ltd., Singapore, 1972, p.1338.

2 Swami Prajanananda (D. Litt.), *Music of the South-Asian Peoples* (Vol.I), 1979, p.1.

To the man, who in pre-historic time first perceived musical sound as it originated in the beating of hollow object or by the swing whirl of a staff, it was something incomprehensible and therefore mysterious and magical. The mere sound of percussion instrument excited him to the pitch of intoxication. From them he discovered the power of rhythm, which inflamed and ordered the ritual dance and also co-ordinated the movements of labour and, as if by magic, lightened the toil.[3] It has been said that music is a language. This seems sufficiently inclusive if one remembers that every language serves to communicate human experiences and aspirations. But just as verbal concepts do not mean the same thing to everyone, so music means different things to different persons at different times. Exactly as language has developed from the communication of simple needs to that of complex and sophisticated meanings, so music has progressed from the conveying of primitive ideas to the expression of subtle shadings of emotion and thoughts.[4]

The music of the Garos is traditional. By traditional we mean, that which is transmitted or handed down from generation to generation, from the teacher to the student. It includes all those ideas, habits or tendencies, techniques, principle and disciplines which are based on experience of the past and are transmitted from one generation to another.[5] This we see in the '*Nokpante*' system (*Nokpante* bachelors' dormitory) of the Garos, where all-round training is imparted to the young men. Here they acquire knowledge in the field of art, craft, carving, music, culture, physical fitness, warfare, defence, medicine, agricultural know - how as well as moral standards and etiquette, which are handed down by skilled elders of the village. Here also, knowledge is imparted on the story of the origin of the

---

3 Einstein Alfred, *A Short History of Music*, London Illustrated Edition, 1953, p.1.

4 Liepman Klaus, *The Language of Music*, U.S.A., 1953, p.1.

5 Swami Prajanananda, *op. cit.*, p.12.

Garos, their mythology, folklore, and tales of the past wars and adventures by the '*Katta agangipa*' (Epic story narrator). Out of centuries of sincere efforts and practices, a marked technique evolves, and out of centuries of experimentations with fixed principle, a tradition comes into being. In music, it means artistic principle and technique, based on unceasing efforts and accumulated experience. Tradition has been aptly described as 'Social heritage' by Thakur Jaideva Singh, one of the connoisseurs of music.[6]

In modern terms, this form of music also falls under what is known as 'folk music'. Different definitions have been given for the term 'folk music'. Pandit Amar Nath opines that "Folk is the condition of music untouched by grammar, untouched by musical science; it is a music which bursts out of a people .... Where these find their origins and where they flow is equally unknown. What is known, is that wherever and whenever hearts beat, there is music."[7] The other is a provisional definition adopted by the International Folk Music Council in 1955, which states that folk music is one that has been submitted to the process of oral transmission. It is a product of evolution and is dependent on the situations of continuity, variation, and selection. Therefore, this term can be applied to music that has been evolved from rudimentary beginnings by a community which is not influenced by art music. Further, it can also be applied to music which has originated from an individual and has thereafter been assimilated into the tradition of the community. But the term does not cover a song/tune/dance that is ready-made and copied unchanged. "It is the fashioning and re-fashioning of music by the community that gives it its folk character."[8] Folk music is, therefore,

---

6 Swami Prajanananda, *Ibid.*, p. 12.

7 Pandit Amar Nath, "The Essence of Folk Music - with reference to Punjabi Music" in *Man and Music in India* , edt. by Dr. Roshmi Goswami, p.50.

8 Percy A. Scholes, *The Oxford Companion to Music*, edited by John Owen, London, Oxford Univ. Press, 1970-75, p.366.

the composition of the race that produces it. It commonly expresses racial characteristics in a very definite way.

It is self-evident that the germ of all music lies in folk music. Every form of vocal and instrumental music we possess has developed out of folk songs or dance, and it is no more possible to make a balanced and comprehensive study of the history of music without an examination of the treasures of folk tunes, than it is to make a similar study of literature without an examination of folk poems and folk tales.[9] There are also echoes of an indigenous music which prevails among the hill tribes, remaining in Indian music today. In every province, go where we will, may be found some melodic or rhythmic habit or turn which it is possible to reckon as proper to it, having its peculiar scale or modes, its figure, rhythm, graces to mark its authenticity.[10] Folk music is generally confined to a particular region and pattern owing to differences of dialect and local tradition.[11] In nature, folk songs are always verse - repeating, they are often in the old modes. The rhythms are often free and the tunes are often related to the composers particular occupation. Prof. John A. Lomax in his '*Cowboy Songs*' (1927) was of the opinion that the sharp and rhythmic yells which were sometimes put into verse were not only used to stir up lagging cattle, but were also used during the long watches of the night guards as they rode round the herd, improvising cattle lullabies which quietened and soothed the animals to sleep. In fact, he stated that some of the best of the so-called 'dogie songs' seemed to have been "created for the purpose of preventing cattle stampede - such songs coming straight from the heart of the cowboys, speaking familiarly to his herd in the stillness of the night."[12]

9 *Ibid.*, p.368.

10 C. Ray, *The Music and Musical Instruments of Southern India and the Deccan*, 1977, p.X.

11 Swami Prajanananda, *op. cit.*, p.13.

12 Percy A. Scholes, *op. cit.*, p.367.

Thus, folk music is not necessarily archaic **and its** making still goes on in less sophisticated communities **where** the conditions of life calls for self-entertainment.

Musical patterns and forms as well as their way of presentation differ from age to age, place to place and from time to time. It has been used by primitive men to please themselves. Their music was known as weather music, agriculture music, cremation music, passion music, wedding music etc. Their music was mainly recitative, but was tuneful though monotonous... It was bounded up with everyday life and with many special factors, psychological, sociological, religious, symbolic and linguistic. J.A. Mac-cullock said that the primitive savage and simple melodies or tunes were never long. They consisted of a few notes (one or two), and a phrase tended to be endlessly repeated. Hans Tischler observed that even among the primitive men, work songs, war songs, ballads, simple ritual dances, and chants were accompanied by rhythm and tempo.[13] Different races tend to develop different song idioms - the use of particular scales, melodic intervals, rhythmic motifs, etc., to some extent these may be the result of chance and of fashion, but in a considerable degree they seem to express the spirit of the race.[14] Alain Danielou opines that - like the forms in language, musical modes are permanent marks of tradition to which people belong. Every where, when artificial systems have not destroyed or disfigured traditional modes, it is as easy by the study of musical modes as by that of linguistics, to observe the migrations and influences of race upon each other.[15] A.J. Hipkins makes a remark that - "from whatever point of view we overlook the human race, its history and development, we can nearly always trace music as having some connection, however slender, with the particular

---

13 Swami Prajanananannanda, *op. cit.*, p.80.

14 Percy A. Scholes, *op. cit.*, p.967.

15 R.C. Mehta, *Studies in Musicology*, Bombay, Baroda, p.94.

form of culture, or it may even be the absence of culture, under notice."[16]

A study of the music of the Garos proves to be not only an eye opener, but also evokes one's deep respect for the ancients who have developed such simple yet intriguingly melodious and varied tunes. The beauty of their music lies in the adaptability of the music to suit an occasion, and the extempore composition of most of these folk songs in their simple yet haunting tunes. Here it is interesting to note that, the first tunes are said to have been picked up by imitating the sounds of nature, such as the wind and water, the different sounds emitted by insects, birds and animals. This view gains support from the words of Darwin, who says that music evolved from the imitation of calls and cries, i.e., the sounds of animals and birds. As Swami Prajanananda says, "sound is the cause as well as the source of music" and music emerged in a gradual process from the hoary past up to the present time. Alfred Einstein supports this view by pointing out that, "Natural science has tried to discover a pre-human origin for music in the song of birds"; and comparative musicology, which deals with prehistoric development of music, has admitted that primitive man may have been attracted by bird songs in the first place and have continued to use it as a model for imitation. Schmidt and Carl Stumf were of the opinion that music of the world evolved like speech from the necessity of giving signals to distant places by sound, and their views also find support from the vedic literature.[17]

Music soon became a part and parcel of the Garo society, and it came to be used in all occasions. It became the main means of expressing their feelings of sorrow, joy, of thanksgiving and adoration; it was used to invoke their Gods and to appease them. Stories and events of their glorious

---

16 C. Ray, *The Music and Musical Instruments of Southern India and the Deccan* (Taken from the introduction given by Hipkins).

17 Swami Prajanananda, *op. cit.*, p.48.

past, heroes and heroines have been related through songs in ballad form. These have been passed down from generation to generation in oral tradition, as there were no written scripts then. The process of oral transmission has been responsible not only for the preservation of folk music, but for the course of its development and in a sense for its actual creation. The richness of Garo music can be seen in its variety. The songs of epic romantic themes, love songs, ballads and lyrics are of many kinds. Being agriculturists, their agricultural ceremonies are initiated by prayer chants and then culminate with social activities of feasting, dancing and singing. This is the time when one is introduced to different forms of music in a relaxed atmosphere. Music was composed to suit the occasion and so we find songs with different lyrics, beat and rhythms, sung to the accompaniment of a variety of musical instruments. The use of Musical instruments depended on the gravity of the situation.

Because of the wide distribution of the people over a vast area, and the distance between the various sub-tribes, each group of people have developed a distinct style of music, instruments and dance. Some of the musical instruments are used only by a particular group. As for example - the type of music most prevalent in the Dual area are: *Rere ring.a, Gonda doka* and *Grapmangtatta.* The first two are used at any time, while the latter is sung only during the *Mangona* ceremony, i.e., the post-funeral ceremony, which takes place a year after a man's demise.

The *Rugas, Garas, Ganchings, Matchis* and *Atongs* on the other hand lay stress on the *Mangona* or *Chugan* ceremony and as such their songs are related to that occasion. The *Atongs* also have the *'Atong Katta'* which is similar to the '*Katta Agana*' of the other areas, which is an epic story narration rendered by the use of a particular tune called '*Kurangma sala'.* The Matchis too have the '*Dani doka*' tune which is sung during the harvest festival and the *Ganna pe.a* or *Jaksil Ganna* ceremony, a ritual by which the *Nokma* or headman used to prove his chieftainship. This custom, however, has practically vanished due to the poverty of the *nokmas* as well as their conversion to Christianity.

The biggest group among the Garos, namely the *Ambengs*, have a great number of songs especially related to their dance music. The songs sung in these areas are the haunting tunes of the *Ahoea, Ajea, Ku.rangma sala, Ajebawilla* and *Doro ring.a.*

Perhaps the area that can boast of having the most melodious tunes with different beats and timings, is the *Chisak* and *A. we* areas which have the *Ohomai, Kore bima, Kore doka, Gosai ring.a, Arowaka, Bowel, Harara, Serejing, Nangorere*, etc.

Songs were the vehicles through which man communicated with one another and with nature which was seen as the very personification of the Gods themselves. For example, *Goera* seen as the God of thunder, *Saljong* the Sun God, as well as the God of food crops and so on. It was the one way by which the history of their past could be kept alive in the hearts and minds of the people from generation to generation. Songs were also used for the renewing of the fertility of the soil and crops, for invoking the spirit - Gods for exhibiting magical feats and even for the curing of diseases.

Folk-tales, myths, songs, prayers and records of the history of the tribe formed the oral literature, of these, songs and prayers each with tunes of their own, may be said to constitute poetry. Prayers are chanted during ceremonies which are connected with various occasions. The prayer follow a particular pattern and though there may be slight differences in the recitation, the substance remains essentially the same. Prayers made during the sacrificial ceremonies for the sick, and at every stage of 'jhum' cultivation and during the betrothal rites performed for a man and a woman, may be cited as examples.[18] Some prayers

---

18 Caroline R. Marak, *Influence of English on Garo Poetry with particular reference to three Authors*, 1985 (Unpublished Thesis) NEHU, Shillong, Meghalaya.

require a priest, others like the prayers during sacrificial ceremonies connected with jhum cultivation may be recited by the head of a family. This type of song is called *Krita* by the Garos.

Garo folk songs can be placed under several basic groups such as, Invocational incantations or *Mite tata, Amua* or *Krita*, songs for social activities and festivals, Lullabies or *Mumua*, Ballads or *Katta agana, Dirges* or *Grap Mangtata.*

CLASSIFICATION OF SONGS

I. Amua, Krita or Invocational Songs Connected with Jhum Cultivation

The invocational songs are monotonous and tuneless chants. The first of such songs we come across during the agricultural cycle is the 'A.a opata' which goes:

> "*Asima Dingsima, Drama, Chisama,*
> *Depema, Denjemani a.dok - chigako,*
> *Anga o.nakengjok, anga wang.nakengjok,*
> *Jamang daknaka, a.dal o.naka, mite Abitpara,*
> *Knapabo, nasongpabao,......*
> *Na.a namnikode, jajumangchi jakarichi aganpinikpabo,*
> *A.a o.patnaka, jumang sipanaka,*
> *A.song rakigipa chiga nirokgipa.*"[19]

The translation says –

> In the land which belongs to *Asima, Dingjema, Droma, Chisama,*
> *Depema, Denjema* (the creator of vegetations),
> I have a mind to clear the jungle for jhuming as *a.dal'* (new jhum field),
> and '*jamang*' (smaller plot, substitute for jhum field).
> *Abitpa*! (care-taker deity) respond to my prayers.
> Reveal to me your consent or disapproval in my dreams,
> Oh! keeper and guardian of the land.

Having chosen the plot, the next step is taken, i.e., the clearing of the jungle. This is known as *Den.bilsia* or *A.a bakchata*, which also signifies the driving off of all

---

19 Mihir Sangma, Private Collection, 1991.

uncleanness and disease. The incantation used at this time goes in this way:

"*A.cho marang, songgimikni madrang,*
A.bimo ro.rengpakchok, bripgipa urigipako,
Dilnauatnaka, diltetatnaka, chri-watalchi,
Bra-kewalchi marangko-starangko,
Bolchuranggoming, Mandal chidominġ, gakatangbo, gadoangbo
Guridimung mikkasiming, gakat mikkasimung, gakatangchina, gadoangchina, daode jabilsi kaket,
A.a bakshatnajok, a.a sonakengjok, kilgukangnakengjok."[20]

The translation is:

Shoo ! Curses of the whole village.
The jungle is over grown with trees and creepers which need to be cleared.
With the help of the bow and arrow and the oar
I will drive away the profanations from the land.
Climb away on the Simul (*Bombax malabaricum*) and the Mandal tree (*Erythina suberisa*),
Go away with the black clouds and fog for the whole year,
For I claim this land for my cotton fields.

This is followed by the jhum burning ceremony called '*Asiroka*', during which the following incantation is used to call up the goddess *Mini Maa Rokime* (the mother of hill paddy) to dwell in their land and bless them with good harvest.

Go..me! knajokma meenmaa Rokime,
Ga.songpaebo, chingni a.bimo ge.motpaebo.
Patiepabo, ra.ronepabo, suakime, kime a.sale,
Gitok a.wite, be.en simrangrang,
Gitok tongjangjang, Arengma Sandomana,
A.kinmanagita, patiepabo, raronepabo."[21]

---

20 Mihir Sangma, *Maniani Bidik*, Garo Hills Book Emporium, Tura, Meghalaya, 1989, p.5.

21 *Ibid.*, p.5.

Go.me! (a form of exclamation) Mother of hill paddy,
I do hereby request you to set foot on my jhum field,
Plant and distribute your blessings on it.
Make this land of *Arengma Sandoma* fertile,
The harvest as plentiful as the crop of termites.

The Garos generally follow multi-crop system, wherein, the various seeds are broadcasted simultaneously. In this way a constant supply of different crops is obtained in batches. The time when the seeds sprout and grow into young shoots is considered the most vulnerable period for the plants by the Garos. Thus they have a special ceremony for this period and it is known as '*Me.jak sim.a.*'

The priest (*kamal*) takes a lump of earth from the field after going around the land, naming the various curses. He puts the lump of earth in a special basket with a lid (*koksep*) and shouts that all the curses and diseases have been put in. Then the prayer is chanted which runs thus –

"*Siroroangnabe, siwajakangnabe, cha.waljoo,*
Ang. a.bimo, ang. a.jao.
Do.sik janggil tangpachina, tangsekgilgil nampachina.
Katangbo, reangbo at..cho! skal."[22]
Do not shrivel and wither away
Within my field and its boundaries.
Let the paddy grow lush and green
Like the green back of the parrot.
Shoo! Be gone you demons.

Having assured the safe growth of the plants, we come to the time of harvest. The first fruits are never eaten but are first given as thanks offering to *Misi Saljong*, the sun god, who first taught man the art of cultivation. This ceremony is called *Rongchu gala* (offering of flattened rice). The ceremony is always initiated by the *Nokma* (Clan Chief). The chants recited at this time say:

22 *Ibid.*, p.8.

"Patigipa, ra.rongipa, ge.songipa, ge.botgipa,
Katchi Beari, Misi Susime.
Cha.patokbo, ringpatokbo,
Nang.na cha.chengjawa, nang.na ringchengjawa.
Gindeko wantiko, nang.ming ringrimgnok, nang.ming cha.rimgnok."[23]

Bestower of blessings, sower and planter,
Katchi Beari (demon) and *Susime* (the Moon God).
Partake of this food and rice-beer
Which we will not eat or drink before you,
But shall have with you.

A special ceremony is performed during the reaping of the jhum paddy. This is called *Ja.megapa* or *Migap ra.rona.* The chants used at this time goes:

"Angna patigipa, angna sualgipa,
Salonakengjok, ra.onangnakengjok.
Gal.a jrignok, gal.paksamaignok.
Angade janggil itnakengjok,
Daode songdongrikaibojok,
Nangnan on.pilgnok, nangnan walpilgnok"[24]

My benefactor ! I am taking away
What you have given me.
I shall leave the land fallow,
That the natural vegetations may spring up again,
The tired land may regain its fertility,
I return it to you.

So in these lines we see that the land will be left fallow so that it regains its fertility. It is interesting to note that, while the sheaves of paddy are being brought in, the children follow the person carrying the sheaves, uttering the words '*Ahoea, Ahoea*'.[25] This is probably the sequel to the sing

23 *Ibid.*, p.9.

24 *Ibid.*, p.11.

25 B.Chaudhury, *Some Cultural and Linguistic Aspects of the Garos*, Lawyers Book Stall, Gauhati, 1958, p.26.

song that takes place in the evening, between the youngmen and maidens of the village. The song that is usually sung is known as *Ahoea*. The verse is sung by one person and the others repeat the refrain.

Finally, we come to the biggest of the festivals of the Garos - the *Wangala* or harvest festival. This is also known by other names such as *Drua wanbola* and *Wanna rongchua*. This is a "Thanksgiving" as well as a "Send-off ceremony" to bid farewell *to Minimaa Kiri Rokime* (Mother of paddy) and *Misi Saljong* (God of food crops) who would return to their respective homelands somewhere in the universe, after the harvest is over. At this time an important ceremony is performed known as "*Kumanchi Wal.dukaa*", which literally means negotiation between God and man, where a special request is made to the Gods to return in the next season.

The cultural aspect of music and dance as a traditional part and parcel of the *wangala* festival, can be traced back to the mystic past related in their mythology. According to their myth, the creator '*Tattara Rubga Stura Pantura Misi Siste*', after the completion of the creation of the heavens, the earth and all beings, which took eight days. He performed the first "*Drua Wanbola*" or *wangala*, in a place called '*Dakgipani a.song Biambini chiga*'. the motive behind which, was to show the supremacy and importance of the creator. All the living things took part in this celebration. The only creatures who could not show up for the feast was man, who was, therefore, ignorant of the rites and rituals of the *wangala* ceremony. *Manepa* - the king of the land and *Sanepa* - the king of the waters had sent two representatives respectively to this first *wangala* celebration, they were *Asi* and *Malja*. On the way, the two humans rested for the night in the jhum field of *Nose* and *Dimse* the sister and niece of *Misi Saljong* respectively. Without permission they dug up some yam and ginger from the field, boiled and ate it, then continued on their journey to the land of the creator. When *Nose* and *Dimse* discovered the theft they reported it to *Misi*

Saljong, who placed a curse on the trespassers. As a result *Asi* was killed by a tiger and *Malja* was taken by a sea serpent. This was the reason for man's ignorance of the rites and rituals of *the Wangala* function.

Fortunately for man, the other creatures were kind enough to teach man in their way, the various rites and rituals. The wagtail bird (*Ajema*) demonstrated the art of dancing by wagging her tail artfully. From the Bulrush plant (*Re.ruma*) man learnt to clap their hands rhythmically. It was a large lizard that lives both on land and water, that first put melon blossoms on its head and showed man the art of decorating the head for the dance. It was from its colourful body that man got the idea of decorating the house with rice powder. The sound of wind passing through the punctured holes in the bamboo (demonstrated by the bumble bee) gave man the idea of playing the flute. Man also picked up tunes from the sweet music made by various creatures like the crickets, birds and animals. Since then, music became the food of love for human beings and dancing the way of life of the people.

It was only after gaining knowledge from all these sources, that man, represented by *Munepa* and *Sanepa*, started the *wangala* ceremony on the surface of the earth. It is on this foundation, that the traditional culture of the Garos have stood the changing tide of time till the present time.

The first of the ceremonies connected with *wangala* is the '*Rugala*' - offering libation to the benevolent gods and goddesses by pouring out rice beer. This is followed by '*Chachat soa*' - burning of incense, which is performed in the *Nokma's* house. The following incantation is used during the *Rugala*:

"Patigipa Ra.rongipa, ge.songgipa, ge.botgipa,
Katchi Beari, Misi Susime.
Cha.patokbo, ringpatokbo, Nang.na cha.changjawa,

Nang.na ringchangjawa.
Gindeko wantiko, nang.ming, ringrimgnok, nang.ming cha.rimgnok."[26]

Giver of all good things, master of cultivation,
Katchi Beari (a demon), as well as *Misi Susime* (the moon god).
I call upon all of you to partake of these first fruits that we offer you.
Let us eat and drink together.

The next day after early lunch, the whole village gathers in the *Nokma's* house for the *Chachat so.a* ceremony. Cooked rice is scattered on the floor of the *Nokma's* house - signifying the falling of hail stones at the beginning of monsoon. This is followed by the burning of incense till the whole room is filled with smoke. The smoke takes the place of rain clouds that gather during the monsoon season. While burning the incense the *Nokma* sings the following incantation:

"Anga cha.chatmikjok, mongchimnajok, sengtoa, similnama.
Agru Mite, Dongkreng Pante, Totmari kinge miko, Doti pagrina on.a.
Nang.nan so.miknajok, nang.nan mongchimnajok."[27]

I have burnt the sweet smelling incense in your honour
Along with sandal wood and resin,
And given food to the orphans.
In your honour I am performing this ritual
And have invited guests to the feast.

The *Nokma* who is dressed in his finery starts to sing the *'Dani doka'* (one form of Garo song) to the ceaseless accompaniment of the *kram* (sacred drum), the Rang or gong, the *Adil* or horn and the *Dama* or long drum. The song goes –

---

26 Mihir Sangma, *Maniani Bidik*, p.9.

27 *Ibid.*, p.9.

"*Oho anga dania*
Oho anga Radaa
Anga dani dokonga,
Chinga rada ring.onga.
Ia nokding Mite,
Ia bolding Katchi.
Mite knabo,
Katchi ra.chakbo.[28]

Oh I'm singing the *dania* (particular song)
Oh I'm doing the *radaa* (play)
Oh I'm beating the *dania* tune,
We're singing the *radaa*
To the house spirit
Spirit of this wood
Hear us oh God
Receive us, spirit.

The *Nokma* then leads the dancers into the '*A.tila*' or courtyard, where various forms of dances are performed. Led by the *Nokma*, every house in the village is visited systematically until the entire village is covered.

Having thus honoured the various gods at the two ceremonies, all that remains is to spend three or four days feasting on the slaughtered cows, drinking rice beer, dancing[29] and singing. Merry-making and socializing begins hereafter. The change in the mood is seen in the light hearted bantering while singing and dancing, among the young and old alike. This is also a time for story telling, especially the mildly competitive stories in which two people alternately chant, each trying to outdo the other in the cleverness and obscurity of his phraseology, to the amusement of the bystander.[30] This particular form of singing is known as

---

28 Mihir Sangma, *Pagitchamni Ku.bisring*, Garo Hills Book Emporium, Tura, Meghalaya, 1982; p.94.

29 Robbins Burling, *Rengsangiri*, University of Pennsylvania Press, 1963, p.65.

30 *Ibid.*, p.67.

'*Doro ring.a*'and it can go on till the wee hours of the morning. The other kinds of songs usually sung during the *wangala* celebration are *Kurangma sala; Ajea* or *Kajea; Ajebawilla; Ahaoea; Dani doka; Ohomai ring.a; Kore doka* or *kore ring.a; Gosai ring.a; Katta agana.* As Gabriel Bertrand experienced, "There was no pause in the continuous polyphonic chanting, in the fine Garo tongue, of the simple ever-recurring melodies, with their alternation of solo and chorus ... It was wonderful to listen to them, now a full throated male chorus, now a sudden silence, now a sustained mezzo-voce to a flute obligato and now drowned in the roll of *tam-tam.*" Maracas made of gourds filled with gravel kept up their strange rattle.

II. **Festival and Social Songs including Love Songs**

Music is not, however, restricted to festivals and celeb-rations for the *A.chik mande* (hill man). It is used at all times and in every situation for the pure pleasure of singing. So we find a variety of catchy, teasing and soothing tunes that reflect every mood of the people. To mention some we have *Doroa*, the *Tantani sul, Kambe ring.a, Gonda doka, Dame ring.a, Aha gogai, Gelo ring.a, Arowaka, rere ring.a* or *Rere kal.a, Direng sola, Rada ring.a, Howa ring.a, Boel, Nanggorere goserong, Serejing, Sonatchi sul, Sonajing, Bisa mumua, Katta agana,* and *Atong katta.* Then they also have the dirges known as *kabe, Manggrapa* or *mangtata.*

Doroa* or *Doro ra.a

Doroa is a form of music which can be adapted for any occasion, the theme depending on the situation. It can be sung as a solo piece or alternately by two people. The latter form proves to be more interesting as it is rendered in a competitive spirit, thus adding spice to the music. According to Pa Jendan Sangma of village Waribokgre, *Doroa* is the basic or original tune. The beauty lies in the impromtu composition of the words by the singers, who pick up where the other has left off, beautifully narrating tales without breaking the link. This form of music is best performed in the evening (Appendix - VII).

Doroa

Dore seko til.eka, Bengbul ja.chok rokreka,
Dore sko chota, Bangbul ja.chok be.a,
Mite bi.sarara, Katchi angderara,
I.na gesebaongana, I.na dokgrikbaongana.
Rong kole gogrikbaonga,
Jaktome dokgrikbaonga,
Rubuga sol.e nipila,
Dakara repe dakpila.
Rabugani sol.jaode, Dakaruni repjaode,
Doreko sol.e nijaode, Bangbulko repe dakjaode,
Dorona jajanapang, wanbolna wakwanapang,
Norode mandede, Dimade Riside.[31]

Dore was untrue to her husband
With Bengbul, whose feet are shaking with fear now,
Dore's head was cut off,
Bengbul's legs were broken.
All the Gods and demons
For their cause have joined the fight,
With stones and fists,

Rabuga looks back with sharpened tools,
Dakaru too is filing his tools.
If Rabuga and Dakaru do not punish Dore and Bengbul,
Noro, Dima and Risi might hesitate to sing the Doroa
Or even to perform the *wangala.*

Kurama sala* or *Kajea

Dangga bima anteka chengchang gachang mikoa,
Moharanai potika pongpang gapang simila.
Gori kasi bandao nomil ja.roroenga,
Chengsi gongmiriao jong.si male roenga,

31 Harendra W., Marak; *A.chik Aganbewalrang*, N.E.H.U. Publication, 1983; p.61.

Sa.ra rotojaoba an.tang nokap o.atang nokcha nape dongginok,
Nomil nitojaoba an.tang nike dongatang sako bika changinok.[32]

Hear the tingle of her coin necklace,
Smell the fragrance of the Mohar-blossom arranged on her hair,
As she gently swings on the reed plant.
See the insect crawling on the slender plant,
Though my yard is small
I've cleared it with my own hands
And built a house on it.
'though my girl may not be a beauty
I love her and have married her.

I. *Ajea*

This is a form of singing which can be rendered by one person or alternately by a male and a female, usually lovers, or by a group of men and women in a competitive spirit. Following are two forms of the music, one in a question/ answer form, the other is a solo piece (Appendix - XV).

<u>Me.asa</u> : *Maia dake arimjok, maia dake salchujok ? Donga na.a chamea, nono na.a gitinga ?*

<u>Me.chik</u> : *Wakmana ringkong pakgale arima, Do.dona pura rongkite salchua.*

<u>Me.asa</u> : *Knasingsangkujama, nikjagringkujama ? Wakmana ringkong doke neng.nenga, Buchuma dangkep ra.e gepgepa.*

<u>Me.chik</u> : *Na.a maina ma.haming, ma.chong aganalboda, Biming maia mingaming, minge mesokkalboda.*[33]

<u>Male</u> : What have you been doing till so late, the sun has already risen so high ? Do you have a lover, little sister ?

32 Mihir N. Sangma, *op.cit.*, p.85.

33 H.W. Marak, *A.chik Aganbewalrang*, NEHU Publication, 1983, p.71.

Female : I got delayed feeding the pigs and the chicks.

Male : Did you not sense my feelings for you ? While I was carving the pigs trough? I entreat you to tell me, Before the old lady takes a tong and comes to chide you.

Female : Which family do you come from And to which clan do you belong ?
What is your name, do tell me please ?

II. ***Ajea* (solo)**

Asiki rongbirong nabajok,
Donga saljong mikchirong sokbajok, nomila danang,
Donggijako do.rengreng ganama, nomila-ha
Chongijako mejareng ramama, nomila-ha
Madosa saa tingkong konga – Hmm
Bani pante oktongtong - Hmm ooo hm
Na moa ma. saming ma.chong
Anganangkuaming nomila – Ha
Bolni jasing kasaming akkego nangkuaming nomila - Ha.[34]

Stars of all colours have appeared
With the appearance of a beautiful maiden
Created by Saljong (Sun God)
Having nothing on except a strip of cloth.
The surplus rice was dried in the sun
By Mado (name of a person), who scrapped it out from the pot.
Whose son is this pot bellied youth ? Ooh Hmm
Which clan do you belong to young maid ?
You who love the trees and are sowing seeds, young lady?

Ahaoea

This is the song of the *Ja.megappa* season, when the paddy has just been cut and are being brought into the granary. However, it can be sung throughout the harvest

34 Donising D. Sangma of Village Me.gapgre; 16.1.92.

season, for it ushers in the time of feasting **and merry-**making.

Nabal gane niksenga, a-hoa, a-hoa.
Sada ra.na gandasa, a-hoa a-hoa,
Jako poisa anasa, a-hoa, a-hoa.
Nomil dongja re.baja, a-hoa, a-hoa,
Damanamja mikoja, a-hoa, a-hoa.[35]

The earring makes me look better,
As I go to buy an anna worth of tobacco a-hoa, a-hoa,
Which is all I have at hand a-hoa, a-hoa.
Haven't come across any maids so far a-hoa, a-hoa,
The long drum makes no sound, its defective a-hoa, a-hoa.

From the words of this song, we come to learn that men too wore earrings.

Dani Doka

Dani is a traditional Garo song sung by the elderly men, to the exclusion of women and young men. While singing the *Dani* one takes the lead in singing the verse, then the others join in responsively, saying '*Ho-anga dania*' or '*Hai-anga dania*' at the end of each line.[36] The singing begins inside the *Nokmas* house and then the crowd moves on to the courtyard, where vigorous dancing and feasting begins, to last for at least three days. The author has come across two forms of singing the *dani*. The theme of the *Dani doka* is usually the myth concerning the origin of the *wangala* dance, as the following words will reveal - (Appendix - I).

Tune-I

Aningchi drenchengbaa
Chiningchi wanbolchengbaa,

---

35 Mihir N. Sangma, *Pagitchamni Ku.bisring*, Op.cit., p.87.

36 Caroline R. Marak, *Influence of English on Garo Poetry with Particular Reference to Three Authors*, 1985 (unpublished Thesis), N.E.H.U., Shillong, Meghalaya, pp.52-53.

Maagipani a.songo
Bidaweni chigao,
Anchengko mande dake,
Kasiko do.me pote,
Duaringko ringringe,
Wa.singtokko tingtoke,
Ku.chi imbingbingbae.[37]

It was in the underworld
The land beneath the waters,
In the land of the mother
And the waters of *Bidawe*,
That the *wangala* was first demonstrated.
A human figure was fashioned out of the mud,
A reed plant fixed on the head.
You could hear the hum of music
To the accompaniment of the bamboo clarinet And the bamboo flageolet.

Tune-II

Oh anga radaa
Oe anga dania
Bima pe.e nina
Skon taru rak.uja
Amako maneko
Ambiko pilteko
Aman brikujana
Chiaricha re.anga
Oh anga ra-daa
Oh anga dania.[38]

Oh I'm doing the *radaa* (play)

Yes I'm singing the *dania* (particular song)

---

37 Harendra W. Marak, *A.chik Anganbewalrang*, NEHU, Publication, 1983, p.71.

38 Mihir N. Sangma, "The Various Forms of Tribal Dances and Music", presented during the Seminar on Festivals and Ceremonies in Meghalaya, 13th & 14th June 1991, Tura, p.4.

The fever should leave
The new born baby.
My little mother, aunt, grandmother, my one and only.
Your ageless mother
Has just gone to the river side.
Oh I'm doing the *radaa*
I'm singing the *dania.*

Ohomai ring.a

There are three different tunes to this song - that of the *Ambengs*, the *Chisaks* and the *A.wes* (Appendix-XIV).

Tune-I (***Ambeng***)

Nok jangchio bawila chima samseng gitchue ohoma
A.ba bara rekuna kurang kna baarok - ohoma
Tusio jumang nikuna chame jadin ba.arok - ohoma.
Regitchini soksola chame jakjippagita ohoma
Gaantini rengrenga jojong girappagita ohoma.[39]

The house is filled with the smell of cockles *ohoma*
Think I'll go to my jhum fields
I might hear my beloveds voice *ohoma*
Maybe if I sleep there my sweetheart might come to me *ohoma.*
The plantain leaves waving in the breeze reminds me of my lover *oho-ma*
The jangling bells reminds me of my brothers cries *ohoma.*

Tune II ***Chisak* and *A.we*)**

Noksamoni Kangkani bite,
Chinga Dira jillani pante ... Ohomai da.ning.[40]

The fruit of the plum tree from the neighbourhood,
A young man from the land of Dira.

39 Chongrin D. Sangma - Travelling minstrel of village Jonchepara, West Garo Hills.

40 Mihir N. Sangma, *op. cit.*, p.4.

Kore Doka* or *Kore Ring.a

This tune is used only by the *Chisaks* and *A.wes*. Here too we find two ways of rendation of the song (Appendix-IV).

Tune-I

Ch : *Kore bima redingko mala,*
A.silika a.ningko bita.

Ragong bolbijak gita,
Do.do dorimit gita,
Nikrikaijok chameko
Salni napangagita – Anga
Chanchi man.a gisiko nang.na.[41]

Ch : The cockroach crawls on the clothes line, The cricket digs the ground.

Like the Eleocarpus robusta leaf,
Like the little yellow bird,
Like the setting of the sun,
I saw my lover go,
You are always in my mind.

Tune-II

A.ba bolritchong gita - kore, kore,
Do.ka manggisimgita - kore, kore.[42]

Like a tree stump in the jhum field - *kore, kore,*
Like the black crow - *kore, kore.*

Gosai Ring.a

This is also a *Chisak A.we* tune, and is versatile in that it can be sung as a solo piece or as a group song. It has a refrain like most of the Garo songs, and it runs thus (Appendix - X):

---

41 *Ibid.*

42 *Ibid.*

Gogai wai, gosai wai direng wai.
A.we joljol bawilna,
Chame anga Goera,
Gando makkal badingna,
Songabate re.bara.

Gogai wai, gosai wai, direng wai (2)
Nokma wangalanasa
Re.baming cha.pana,
Siru a.palanasa, bilbaming goserong.[43]

I, the brave, go along the plains, indeed,
I go from village to village,
In order to challenge other men
For a fight, indeed.

I have come to join in the *Nokma's wangala*,
To join in the feast, indeed,
When I saw the wide native umbrella
I literally flew in, indeed I did.

Tantani sul

Tantani is one of the earliest tunes used by the Garos (Appendix – XIX):

Nasimangde pagiri,
Nasimangde magiri,
Na.mang biranganade,
Anga duk ong.chaka,
Angko Tantan mingake,
Angan nang.ni mahari,
Na.simangni manderang,
Malbok bok balbokni,
An.chengbok silsokni.[44]
You have no father,
You have no mother,

43 Lewellyn, R. Marak, Personal Collection, 1988, Tura.

44 Julius L.R. Marak, *Serejing Aro Waljan*, Ri-Khasi Press, Shillong-1, 1988, p.13.

I feel sad to see you lost.
My name is Tantan,
And I belong to your clan,
I come from the land
Where the *Malbok* plantain grows,
And where the sand is white.

Gonda Doka

The *Gonda* tune is said to have come after the *Tantani* tune and there appears to be two or three versions of it. This is a peculiarity of the *Dual* area and can be sung as a solo piece or in alternation by a male and a female singer (Appendix - II).

Tune-I

Gonda maria
Badu maiko chanchia.[45]

What does Badu think about
My rendation of the *Gonda* song.

Tune-II

Gongminaba gongchidok,
Gong.sakosa dakgine,
Do.sioba magina,
Do.sa searingine.[46]

The jews harp costed sixteen rupees,
Its not worth the price,
Its no use performing the marriage sacrifice,
The poor hen is killed unnecessarily.

Tune-III

Mechik : *Smil smil agalmak dongja kile onpana,*
Salrakako chaknamja sawa jamdap rikpana.

---

45 *Ibid.*, p.13.

46 Mihir N. Sangma, Personal Collection, 1992, Tura.

Mea : *Balwa balsri balao neng.takebo dikdiksa, A.ko gamna nangoba gamna an.ching chamesa.*[47]

Female : The burnt jhum produces sweet smell, But there's no one to give me the cotton seeds. I cannot stand the heat of the sun, Who will help me to build the jhum house?

Male : Come and rest awhile and enjoy the cool breeze,
If we must till the ground We shall do it together my love.

Araowaka

This is a song for any occasion and has a lively, catchy tune. It is sung in the Chisak area of the Garo Hills. The refrain appears to be an imitation of some bird sound (Appendix - V).

Bibal rimit balgipa - araowaka
A.sarini besual - araowaka
Songgipino dongoba - araowaka
Gisikode da gual - araowaka.[48]

The beautiful yellow blossom - *araowaka*
Is the mustard flower - *araowaka*
Though you live in another village – *araowaka*
Please do not forget me – *araowaka*

Rere Ring.a

This form of music is found only among the Dual people. It is sung on joyous occasion by young people, through which they tease each other (Appendix - VI).

Ha-re-re Ha-re-re

Oh nang.ko sati wingana (2)
Nokma ine donginok (2)

47 Lewellyn R. Marak, Personal Collection, 1992, Tura.

48 Mihir N. Sangma, Personal Collection, 1992, Tura.

Nokcha sokangjokode
Anggitaan dilpanok,
Ha-re-re ha-re-re.[49]

Oh I mistook you for a chief
Because of your umbrella,
Back home I'm sure
You're as poor as me
Ha-re-re ha-re-re

Howa sul or ring.a (Appendix – XX)

Howa-ra-ra, Howa-ra-hia (2)
Songko nokko bilgipa dosik,
Howa-ra-ra howa-ra-hia
Angni mikchagipara me.chik.
Howa-ra-ra howa-ra-hia.[50]

Howa-ra-ra, Howa-ra-hia (2)
The parrot which flies past the house
Howa-ra-ra, Howa-ra-hia
Is my lady love
Howa-ra-ra, Howa-ra-hia

Boel ring.a (Appendix – VIII)

Nitogipa pul baona balenggipa pulrang,
Gitchak rimit nitoriri ma.dimenggiparang
Chel.aode man.gen gita nika nangko rim.na,
Re.angode bile kata kene ang jagringna.[51]

Beautiful flowers blooming in shades of red and yellow,
From a distance you seem within reach
But when I approach, you fly away in fear of my shadow.

Nangorere goserong

A song for all happy occasions, the verses are sung

49 *Ibid.*
50 Julius L.R.Marak, *Serejing Aro Waljan*, p.14.
51 *Ibid.*, p.17.

alternately by young men and women singly or in chorus. This is a favourite of the males. However, there is no logical progression of thought from one verse to another, because most verses are self contained and are not continuations or replies to the previous ones (Appendix - XII). The song has a refrain which may be translated thus –

Indeed it is so (2)
Yes, indeed it is so.[52]

1. *Donga a.song Baghmara*
Joka simsang chibima,
Rona biap an.senga,
Pagitchamrang songdonga.

Ch : *Nangorere goserong*
Nangorere goserong,
Oe nango goserong. (2)

2. *Gando jaksigniko*
Umang jakalchengana,
Bara ampak dokako
Umang jakalchengbaana.[53]

1. In the land of *Baghmara*
Flows the river *Simsang,*
In this beautiful land
Our forefathers first settled.

Ch : Indeed it is so (2)
Yes, indeed it is so.

2. They first wore just a loin cloth,
Which they made out of beaten bark,
This is what they first used.

---

52 Caroline R. Marak, *Influence of English on Garo Poetry with Particular Reference to Three Authors*, 1985 (unpublished Thesis), N.E.H.U., Shillong, Meghalaya, p.90.

53 As sung by Changrin D. Sangma of Village Jongchepara, West Garo Hills, 16.1.92.

Sonatchi sul

This is essentially a tragedy sung to the *Boel* tune. In this particular piece we can trace the influence of the plains, as the person who sings it to me, lives in the area bordering Bangladesh (Appendix - XIII).

1. *Atchiaoni bimung dona angko Soinabali*
   Baba angko dontaiaha danang Sonatchide.
2. *Songa Patalgiri songni Jarong nokman bisa,*
   Rona namma niwatesa chiring sapuresa.
3. *Ian daka kusin salko angko gimaatjok,*
   Malsin chandra gose angako sambisiko on.e.[54]

1. At birth I was named Soinabali,
   But my father later changed it to Sonatchi.
2. Daughter of the Nokma Jarong of Patalgiri village
   A delightful place with a crystal clear stream running through it.
3. I lost those beautiful days
   Ever since Malsin Chandra poisoned me with some herbs.

Serejing

This particular song is popular with the Garo maidens rather than the boys. There are more than one type of tune to this particular music. The tune has developed from the very primitive, when it was sung to the accompaniment of bamboo and wooden sticks, to the more recent version. The theme also changed according to the advancement of the music. At times there is no linkage between the lines. Initially, the main theme was the flora and fauna, the streams, rivers and hills. There are about six different tunes.

Tune-I (Appendix – XXI)

A.kol cho.panakode cholne,
Uijoade donaibo chame.

54 *Ibid.*

Sakchi bildo gipade do.ma
Na.ara ka.saengama angna ?

You can help dig a hole if you want
But if you're ignorant, leave it my love.
The one who's flying above is a wild goose,
Are you in love with me ?

<u>Tune-II</u> (Appendix – XXII)

Ramaaona do.bisa
Rimbarama rim.baja?
Nangni segit chamnasa
Ka.pakama ka.pakja ? Aiao!

To the road side
Did you bring the chick,
What about your ex-husband
Do you miss him still or not? Oh dear!

<u>Tune-III</u> (Appendix – XXIII)

A.bri a.chu simdimdim,
Aiwa nikatgipanchim
Aman angko jonomram
A.song rengdegatram chim - Aiao!
Hills and mountains dark
Out yonder I can see,
There's where *Ama* (mother) gave birth to me,
That land which is hilly, oh dear!

<u>Tune-IV</u> (Appendix – XXIV)

Amara siangjokna
Angni choneng mitingon;
Appa angko palana,
Aman' sianjamano, aiao!

Mother had passed away
When I was still small,
My Father sold me off
Soon after mother's death, oh dear!

Tune-V (Appendix – XXV)

Appara rang ko.sana,
Merong jakhep gnina
Angko pale chaana,
A.chik kotip kingsana, aiao!

My father, for half a *rang* (Gong)
For two handful's of rice,
Sold me off
For one *A'chik* turban.

Tune-VI (Appendix – XXVI)

Chisamoni samrin.aksalna
Sikirepginok,
Oe rade wal.jande
Angko gisik ra.eng nok, aiao![55]

From the river side
Pull out smooth leaved herbs
And grind them.
Oh yes Waljan must be
Thinking of me, oh dear!

Chera sola

Chera sola is sung only in the *Gara-gan.ching* area. The subject of this particular music is usually the heroes and heroines of old like *Jingjang, Nongdu a.ding pante, Gangga* and *Rutha* (Appendix - III).

Aio ! Jingjang a.songde,
Nangoljani a.jade,
Noking hajalsni banga,
Bi.sa tasisni jela unode.[56]

O dear ! Jingjang's country
The land of Nangal

55 Julius L.R. Marak, *Serejing Aro Waljan*, Op. cit., pp.14-18.

56 Mihir N. Sangma, Personal Collection, 1992, Tura.

Has seven hundred households
And tens and thousands of children.

Harara

This is sung in the *Chisak, A.we* area. (Appendix - IX)

Bol gongding gongdangko
Sol.ja anga nanggiri,
Mamatangni rimjaode
Re.ja anga chawari - Harara, harara.

A.brioni Me.ako
Ranggol Peechaangjok
Agni mikchagipako
Jawa seke katangjok
Harara, harara.

Chiringoni rongpileng
Pile pile gamana
Angni mikchagipako
Jawa seke katanga
Harara, harara.

Wa.naruni kambeo,
Domaski manggni,
Ia songni pantede
Namnambea sakgni - Harara, harara.[57]

I'm not going to pare
The crooked wood,
If my uncle doesn't take me
I won't become the son-in-law.

The bamboo shoot from the hill side
Have all been plucked by the monkey,
My lover has been whisked away by another
Harara, harara.

As the pebbles in the stream turn around

57 *Ibid.*

As I cross the stream
So too I keep turning
To see my lover as I go.

I can see two mapies
Sitting on the bamboo,
I see two handsome men
In the nearby village.

Dimdimdimchang

A song depicting the *wangala* festival, and mentioning all the accessories, fineries needed for the festive occasion. We get an insight into the form of socializing that is done at this time (Appendix - XVII).

Refrain:

Dimdimdimchong dadichong
Dama dokato,
Nomil pante mesaa
An.ching wangalo,
Dama bangsi sikana
An.ching mesana.

1. *Kotip gital ra.ako kae nipana*
Bilsin gisep changsasan, an.senge nina.
2. *Matchu chara milako jengo gatako,*
Cha.e mesae an.sengna an.ching wangalo.[58]

Refrain:

Dimdimdimchong dadichong, (imitation of the drum beat)
We play the long drum
Maidens and young men
Dance the *wangala* together in gay abandon
To the accompaniment of drums and flute.

1. I'll use my new turban to bind my head,
Since this occasion comes just once a year.

58 L.R. Marak, Personal Collection, 1993, Tura.

2. We shall enjoy the fattened calf,
   Eat, drink, and make-merry,
   During this *wangala* season.

Him angai

This song reveals to us, the ability of the Garos to express feeling, through the use of undulating notes and sighs at the end of each verse (Appendix - XI).

1. *Dorimitko nikoba, bibal rimit baloba,*
   Na.a angni sambao, apsan nikpaosaming,
   Inmana, him...angai.
2. *Da.a salde antin sal, anti dokra kenajok,*
   Bi.sa nang.ko niksoe, dingding ka.dingsognok.
   Inmana, him...angai.[59]

1. The beautiful yellow bird and the yellow flower gives me no pleasure
   All because you are not beside me to share my joy.
2. Today is market day so I'll take my bag and go,
   My child will be bursting with smiles when he sees you.

Dime ring.a

This is a speciality of the *Atong* area. It is sung after the *mangona* (funeral) ceremony amidst dance, gaiety and music. This particular song, however, is not confined to *mangona* only but can be sung at any time. Like the *Nangorere* each verse of *'Dime ring.a'* consists of four lines with alternate rhymes. The response may be given by any member of the opposite group. The following song is sung by a young man -

Sami amipang jakstit?
Amipang salmokgeri,
Niwatoka kapaka,
Seko kalsranggiri.

Whose sheaf of thatching is this?
I shall pull off the thatching grass;

59 *Ibid.*

Though I have a good view (of her village)
I feel her absence deeply,
(So) I shall run away with her.[60]

III. **Lullabies**

Bi.sa Mumua

Here is a typical lullaby song sung in the days of old, by the mother or any person carrying the baby on the back with a *Debra* or tying cloth (Appendix - XVI).

Oe-o-de-o-oe-o

Ranggirani takraka, oe-o,
Awa angjong teraka, oe-o (3)
Chamil gongdang mesenga, oe-o,
Deba gnang seenga, oe-o (3)[61]

My little brother there is as sweet, oe-o,
As the yam from the Ranggira hills, oe-o (3)
The pamelo fruit is rather sour, oe-o,
My child too smells like he's wet, oe-o. (3)

Bisa Dingdinga (*Bisa* means baby and *dindinga* means rock)

Dingding ta.mara rongbola nonoa dingding,
Ringdipea dambola dingding.[62]

Radaringgita robone nonora dingding,
Song.a mewaringkoba song.bone dingding.

Rock to sleep my dear round little sister *dingding* (rock)
As I sing and rock you my chubby *dingding*,

60 Caroline R. Marak, "Festivals and Ceremonies of Attongs", presented during the Seminar on Festivals and Ceremonies in Meghalaya; 15th & 16th June 1992, conducted by the Department of Arts and Culture, Govt. of Meghalaya.

61 Mrs. D. Marak, Personal Collection, 1993, Tura.

62 As sung by Jadi Ch. Sangma of Village Boldoringgre, West Garo Hills, 11.1.92.

Like a gentle boat on which you sit *dingding.*
Please cook some bamboo shoot today *dingding.*

IV. **Epic story narration in ballad form**
Katta agana or Katta doka

Katta agana literally means Epic story narration, and *Katta doka* means Epic story moulding. The narration is done by the *Katta agangipa* (native poet cum minstrel) who chants out romantic epic themes of ancient days, and of events long pasts, recounting in an elevated grand style the varied lives and mightly deeds of heroes and heroines like *Dikki, Bandi, Giting* and *So.re.* Of the manners, customs, ways of living and thinking, love and hate, peace and war, of the colourful past of the Garos, when man possessed supernatural powers.

Katta agana is of different varieties depending on the tonal manner of singing or modulated chanting. These varieties of *katta agana* are known as *Dikkotchua; Ring.badria; Katchi doka* or *Katchi ring.a; Dilamandea or A.beng katta; Ruga katta; A.we katta; Saling ring.a* or *Chisak katta*; and *Ring.dikgita.*[63] There is a legendary belief among the *A.chiks* that, the genuine, unalloyed and the most superb *Katta agana*, known as *Katta janggi* or *Saling bireng asol*, can never be taught or sung to anyone who is below fifty years of age; that there must be limited number of listeners, who must be above fifty years. Violation of this restriction brings about total blindness to both the singer and the listener.[64] These poems are not composed extempore but have been handed down from generation to generation by oral tradition. Its origin dates back to the mystic past. The language is archaic, and when translated, loses its depth and beauty. The narration starts with praises for the country of the mother *Dikki*, which is considered the noblest, most glorious,

63 Dewansingh S. Rongmuthu, *The Epic Lore of the Garos*, Department of Tribal Culture and Folklore Research, University of Gauhati, 1967, p.2.

64 *Ibid.*, pp. 2 & 3.

the strongest, best country in the world. Reference is then made to the country of *Duraracha Gitingpa*, the father of *Giting*; the country of the *Matchamaa* - ruler of the *matchadu* or tigers; the sacred place of worship; country of the celestial sisters of *Dikki* and other relations. The neighbouring countries are also mentioned. Unending praises are then showered upon the famous brothers *Dikki*, *Bandi* and *Balwa*. *Dikki*, the son of *Characha* and *Mune* is portrayed as an ideal warrior, statesman, saint and philosopher. *Bandi*, the son of *Chinaracha* and *Gritgenda*, is the bravest and most alert of warrior. *Balwa*, the son of *Doparancha* and *Sahni*, is the fleetest and the most handsome man in the world. The unusual way in which *Dikki* and *Bandi* meet and wed their respective beautiful wives, *Giting* and *So.re*, is romantically elucidated, followed by the duels faced by the braves. The song concludes with the happy and beautiful scene of prosperous family life of the heroic couples.[65]

The "Epic Story Narration" is sung to a modulated tune by a minstrel. At intervals the singer stops and keeps silence, to find out whether his listeners have fallen asleep, because singing generally takes place at night. When a listener responds, saying "*Hai*", the singing is resumed. Two minstrels may also be engaged in narrating the story responsively.

The poem may be sung during periods of leisure at any place. It is usually sung at night in the village, while passing the night at market places or in camps for relaxation and entertainment (Appendix - XVIII).

Extract from the Song "In Praise of the Land of *Dikki's* Mother":-

Rangsilga ahari
Salgrani angde,
Dohbilgani bisa,
Salnima navaram,
A.nima ku.angram,

65 *Ibid.*, p.160.

Chimma tapturam,
Do.de nokgacholram,
Dangga mrong su.suram,
Sonaganthong galram,
Dangga sa.raroram,
Noksam sona barnram.

The heavenly central land,
The child of *Salgra*, the God of Light,
And of the high one,
The land of the Rising sun,
Where waterfalls drip,
Where the earth yawns,
And peacocks peep at doors,
The country of silver pillars,
Where bullions of gold are piled,
Where the rich stroll about the village streets,
Where bars of gold lay stacked up by the homestead;

Extract in Praise of the Land of *Duraracha Gitingpa*, the Matrilineal Uncle and Father-in-Law of *Dikki*:-

Methongramni a.song
Song jatchini gittim,
Sa.ra thangka goram,
Sona so.bok ongram,
Minia cheksi onram.

The country of *Methongram*
The centre of home lands,
Where silver coins are thrown up on village streets,
And gold blooms in the form of banana flowers,
Where the mother of rice bends down.
In praise of *Dikki*:

Dikki dangga mrong
Thodik sona ganthong;
Dikki Mithdei changsa,
Thodik sabo paksa;

Dakdamean dakrima,
Rarimean rurime.

Dikki, the shining pillar of lustrous silver,
Thodik, the glowing bar of gold;
Dikki, the living demi-God,
Thodik, the occult-savant;
Is himself moulded along with *dakdame*,
The goddess of vitality and strength,
And along with *Rurime*, the goddess, who moulds human forms.

In praise of *Bandi*:

Ka..Bandi goera
Silang pattal janera,
Bako dakgijagipa
Maiko man.gijagipa.

Hail *Bandi* like the Thunder god
Who overcomes high places slippery as glass,
What has he not achieved
What has he not conquered.

The narration of the whole story takes about a full nine hours and twenty-seven minutes, according to Dewansingh Shangma Rongmuthu, as sung to him by Jangban Shangma Rongmuthu of village Rongrikimgiri on 16th June, 1958.

V. Dirge

Grapmangtatta or Kabe or Grapmikchi

This music is part of the Mangona or funeral ceremony of the *Atongs, Rugas, Chiboks, Duals* and *Matchis*. They give much importance to the proper bidding of farewell to the departed soul. *Grapmangtatta* literally means lament - it is a funeral dirge. The funeral dirge is a recital of the merits of the departed, as well as a prayer for him (or her) to reach his goal without mishap.[66] The Dirge is sung mainly by the

66 Gabrielle Bertrand, *Secret Lands where Women Reign*, London Robert Hale Limited, 63 Old Brompton Rd. S.W.7, 1958, p.102.

older women of the community. One women continues the song from where the other stops, never losing the musical strain or the rhythm, as they keep a night long watch over the mortal remains of their kith and kin. The stories of the deeds of valour and fame, of the pinnacle of glory reached by their sons and spouses, escape from the mouths of these Garo women who have never learnt to spell their own names. Young and old alike, they have kept the legacy alive by word of mouth.[67]

Ang re.jak dikkia apara,
Ang sati a.wea do.mara,
Memang masal charamo cha.angbo,
Matchu boldak karamo ka.angbo,
Kimdi rakgipagita apara,
Bolsal den.gipagita do.mara,
Stil rong.misina mriari chakaming,
Balwa balmisina gongdole roaming.Ma.na chakgipa saming apara,
Nono kinggipasaming do.mara.[68]

You my son were like the palm leaves
An umbrella my beloved son,
On your way to the spirit land
Take your meal in the resting place of the spirits,
Tie the bull to the (*Schima wallichii*) tree.
You were as strong as the *Misna ferrera* tree,
Your mother and sister you were sheltering my child,
Against the storm and hail stones my beloved.

67 Brucellish K. Sangma, "The Contribution of Garo Women to Garo Literature", an article in the Souvenir Magazine of the 'Mothers' Union Golden Jubilee', 1941-1991, Tura, 1991, p.53.

68 Mihir N. Sangma, Personal Collection.

3

CLASSIFICATION OF MUSICAL INSTRUMENTS

The varieties of devices used to make music are called musical instruments. According to the material, nature and the sound produced, the instruments are broadly classified into four major groups:

1) Idiophones (Greek word - self-sounding) which are made of resonant materials, such as metal or wood, which vibrate and give out notes when struck, for example, Bells, Gongs, Cymbals (metal), and Xylophones (wood and bamboo).

2) Aerophones or wind instruments, whose notes come from air vibrating inside a pipe or tube made of metal or wood, when the tube is blown in different ways, the enclosed air column is set in motion. Under this we have the flutes, whistles, trumpets and horns. Flutes are blown across a hole. The airstream hits the opposite edge of the holes, which vibrates and sets the air inside the tube vibrating. Fipple flutes work on the principle of a whistle. The player blows into one end, and the airstream hits a sharp 'lip' formed by the angled edge of a square hole cut in the side. Reed instruments on the other hand have mouth pieces attached to one end with one or two reeds, usually made of bamboo. In fluted and reed instruments, different notes are

produced by covering and uncovering finger-holes in the tube to make the air column longer or shorter. In trumpets, horns, and other brass instruments, the player's lips take the place of a reed. The end of the tube is held against the lips and the lips are vibrated against the mouthpiece.

3) Chordophones or stringed instruments include Harps, Violins, Banjos and Guitars. Their notes come from the vibrations of stretched strings, which are plucked, strummed, struck or stroked with horsehair attached to a bow. The strings are usually stretched over or have one end attached to a hollow wooden sound box, which makes the sound louder.

4) Membranophones or Drums, have skins or membranes stretched over a frame, as in the Tambourine, or over the ends of wooden or metal cylinders, as in the three major types of drums (kettledrum, snare drum and brass drum). They are played by striking the skins with the hand, with sticks or with soft-headed mallets.

Simple versions of the main types of instruments appeared early in musical history. The first stringed instruments developed from the hunting bow. The mouths of clay pots and the open ends of hollowed pieces of tree trunks were covered with animal skin to make the first drum. Flutes were made of bamboo, and trumpets out of animal horns.[1] They used fibres of palm leaves, grass or entails of the animals for strings of their crude musical instruments of lute type.[2] The materials of which musical instruments are made are the most part those that are found readiest at hand in the country - bamboo, or some similar cane, and

1 *Modern Century Illustrated Encycloepedia,* (Vol. 14); McGraw-Hill Far Eastern Publishers Ltd., Singapore, 1972, p.1343.i

2 Swami Prajnanananda, *Music of the South-Asian Peoples,* (Vol.I), Ramakrishna Vedanta Math, Calcutta, 1979, p.82

large gourds are much employed. These gourds are used for many purposes, and the best are trained in their growth to the shape for which they are required.

A musical instrument to be of any real practical good, requires in its construction not only skilled labour, but experimental knowledge on the part of the maker of the principles acoustics;. he must know of the best materials and the best known methods of building up an instrument from these materials. Such knowledge as this can only be attained by much study and the experience of a regular apprenticeship to the art.[3]

From ancient times to the beginning of the modern period, craftsmanship in musical instruments reached high levels in many parts of the world.[4] Many of the traditional instruments, inspite of their simplicity, prove to be extremely effective musical instruments, and in them we can see the origin of many of the sophisticated instruments of today, which have been improved upon from generation to generation.

Before developing the skill and knowledge of using instruments, the Garos too accompanied songs with the clapping of hands, stamping of feet, whistling and by blowing tunes through certain types of leaves. Gradually, they learnt to use the natural and abundant supply of foliage, wood and bamboo in ingenious ways, along with the horns, hides and entails of animals. Their technological skills and knowledge enable the Garos to draw sustenance from the natural environment in which they live. In fact the bamboo has become so much a part of the Garos that they cannot imagine a country without the bamboo.

These musical instruments can be placed under the four broad classifications mentioned earlier.

---

3 C.R. Ray, *The Music and Musical Instruments of Southern India and the Deccan*, pp.100-101.

4 *Modern Centruy Illustrated Encyclopedia*, Vol.14, McGraw Hill Far Eastern Publishers Ltd., Singapore, 1972, p.1343.

I. **Idiophones**: Under the Idiophones we have the *Rangs* (Gongs) of various sizes, the largest being *Rangkilding* (Gong on a thread), *Rangbong* (fat Gong), Cymbals of various types like the *Kakwa, Nenggilsi, Guri Do.amik* and *Kamal Jakmora*[5], *Gaanti* (big bell), *Susuak*, or *Ja.srang* (anklet bells), *Silcha* (tambourine), *Chigring* or Zither and *Dimchrang* or *Kimjim*.

Gongs vary according to metal and workmanship, and range in price from cheap ones worth only a few rupees to elegant ones worth several hundreds. Garos recognise more than a dozen kinds, measuring anywhere from perhaps a yard in diametre down to no more than a few inches, and variously made of iron, brass or bell metal. Some of the finest gongs are decorated with engraved outlines of elephants, tigers, snakes and other animals. Most of them including the ordinary ones that are beaten at festivals, are more or less basin-shaped and can be held by one rim and struck on the bottom. The most valuable gongs are never beaten but only displayed at the *Wangala* festival. A Gong worth several hundred rupees is an extremely valuable piece of property to a Garo, who can hardly hope by wage labour to earn more than two rupees in one day. Like other heirlooms they can be cashed in if the family runs into difficulties, but heirlooms are sold only at infrequent intervals and with great reluctance. Garos reckon the rise and fall of families by the numbers of gongs they are able to buy or are forced to sell.[6] To all appearance these gongs, which are always of the same pattern, are nothing more than very ordinary basins with flat bottoms and narrow rims, made of brass. They do not possess the rich tones of the Burmese gongs, and to the European mind are entirely worthless. However, to a Garo they have great value. A man's social

5 Llewellyn R. Marak, "Vanishing Forms of Tribal Musical Instruments", Paper presented at the Seminar on Tribal Dance and Music, 13-14 December, 1991, Tura, p.8.

6 R. Burling, *Rengsanggri*, Philadelphia, University of Pennsylvania Press, 1963, p.206.

standing is often measured by the number of *rangs* (gongs) that he possesses. A dead *Nokma* is laid out before cremation on rows of these gongs, and in cases of dispute in which the headmen have to adjudicate, the fine, when one is inflicted, is always of so many rupees and so many *rangs*. After a man's death, it is often the custom to break a hole in the bottom of one of the metal gongs of which he was the owner, and to place it on a stick close to his *Kima* or memorial post.[7]

According to legend, in the beginning *Rabuga* (Progenitor of man) first made *rangs* (gongs) out of clay and tried to sell it in the land of *Susime* (goddess of Moon). But the men in the *a.kang* (market) rejected it outright because it did not emit enough sound and it broke easily. Feeling greatly disappointed and ashamed *Rabuga* was returning home with a drooping head when he was met by *Katchi a.ning* (spirit of the underworld) who felt sorry for him and told him to rest in his *Nokpante* (Bachelors' Dormitory). In his dream the spirit revealed to him the skill of smelting metal and to make them into *rangs* *"Mulko ping-e nibo, Gaminchiko tinge nibo, rue nibo"*[8] (cover the bellows and see, strike the metal and see, heat and pour it out and see). Next morning when he went to wash his face in the stream the shrimp showed him a gleaming object in the water which was the ore from which man first made metal. It was the bat who showed man how to use a bellow by flapping its wings. Thus according to Garo legend, this is how man first discovered metal and made *rangs* and other steel instruments and implements of war (Plate-I).

Under this, we also have the *chigring* (Zither) made out of bamboo. The portion between the two knots of the bamboo are taken. The skin on one side of the bamboo is sliced off on the top; lengthwise very carefully. A square hole is

7 A. Playfair, *The Garos*, London, 1909, p.44.

8 Lelwellyn R. Marak, *op. cit.*, p.2.

punctured in the centre converting the bamboo into a sound box. Four or five strings of skin of the bamboo are then cut on the sides and mounted on crude bridges made of bamboos pieces. These bridges are fixed on both ends of the strings. In order to create tension the strings are tied with bamboo ropes on each end of the *chigring*. Just above the hole, a flat strip of bamboo which is split half-way on both sides, is fixed in such a way that it holds the first two immediate strings in place, and is used to keep time. This instrument is played by holding it between the knees and the chest. Two sticks are used to strike the string and the thumb for keeping the time. A tiny hole is bored on one side, to keep the sticks in when not in use. This *chigring* is very much like that of the other South-Asian Zither called *Tlaipi* (Plate-II). According to Agat Sangma of village Selbalgre, this instrument was the forerunner of the drum. It was from this, that man got the idea of making a drum out of logs, to get a louder sound. The *Atongs* on the other hand believe that the *Chigring* originated from the practise of head hunting. It was the only instrument used in the 'Den *malua*' ceremony (*Den* meaning cut down and *Malua* meaning sneak or lay in ambush), where it was required to sacrifice a head in great secrecy. Having succeeded in acquiring one, the victory dance was conducted with the muted sound of the *Chigring*. Interestingly enough, the dance performed at this time was unlike any, because it was simply the dance of the 'Point finger' called '*Jaksi detingtinga*'.

Then we come to the *Kimjim* or *Dimchrang* of South Garo Hills. This instrument is made solely out of cane. About thirty matured cane sticks of 29 in. are intricately bound together by cane strips in the fashion of a mini-raft. The skin of the cane on the side is then cut into strips without cutting through, and both ends are mounted on long bridges to create tension. The thickness of the strings gave the strings its different keys or notes. Two bamboo sticks are fixed on the back of the *Kimjim* between the strips of cane to give the bass note. A loose cane string is tied between the two bridges on both sides of the *Kimjim.* This is held together by the musician between the thumb and the middle finger of the right hand, and the strings are strummed or plucked by the pointing finger. The timing is kept by the left hand by striking the back strings of the *Kimjim.* This is very similar to the Lyres of ancient Greeks, Assyrians and Hebrews, now long obsolete, a fore-runner of the harp. The Lyre was in effect a small harp, but differed from the normal harp in two essential particulars - the strings were stopped (by the left hand) and it was played not with fingers but with a plectrum on the right hand. *Kimjim* is also held on the knees. It is used while singing the *chera sola* and during all the *Mangonas* (post-funeral ceremony) (Plate-III).

II. **Aerophones**: These are wind instruments of the Garos who initially used *Bolbijak* or leaves. Later they developed more sophisticated forms of wind instruments like a variety of *Bangsi* or flutes and *Adil* or trumpet and *Singa* or horn. It was from nature that man is said to have first heard and learnt to make a flute. On a windy day the wind passed through the holes in the bamboo thus emitting music. It was the *Bambaneng* (Bumblebee) that demonstrated to man the art of drilling holes in the bamboo. The different types of flutes of the Garos are the *Bangsi Mande* with three stops and a figure of a man fixed on top. *Bangsi* the slimmest of the flutes with three stops; *Olongma* is a somewhat bigger flute with three stops; *Bangsi rori* with six stops and *Illep* or *Ilip* which is more of a fipple flute as it is blown with the help of a 'lip' in the blow-hole; *Dakok* is a big flute as long as the arm with one stop only with a square mouth piece and a tiny hole at the other end, Dugong a kind of bugle made of two bamboos, *Duaring* (Clarinet), *Otekra*, a big bamboo flute a yard long and one inch in diameter with only two finger holes; the *Tlara* or *Taragaku* with one stop in the centre and the *Imbanggi* or *Imbingi* is of the nature of a flageolet. It is constructed out of a short piece of thin bamboo, closed at one end and open at the other. The outer hard covering of the bamboo is peeled off, leaving the softer white part below. The mouth-piece is a square hole about half an inch from the top of the closed end. From the mouth-piece downwards a small slip or tongue is cut in the upper surface of the bamboo, by slitting it down on both sides to a distance of about half an inch[9] (Plate-IV).

The *Adil* is a kind of trumpet made out of the top six inches of a buffalo's horn to which a long bamboo mouth-piece is attached. According to the legends passed down, *Rawil Racha* collected the skin and horns of buffaloes and went to *A'ning Bokjare Chining Dimjare Nore Chire*, Who dwelt in the subterranean region, and asked her to teach him to prepare shields and trumpets out of these skins. She told him that, in preparing shields and trumpets he should look at the leaves of the *kochoos* (*Colocasia indicum*) for the shape and then to imitate the stars in decorating them. Thereupon, *Rawil Racha* returned to his village and prepared the first *Danils* (shields) and *Adils* (trumpets) as instructed.[10]

The *Singga* is the whole of the buffalo horn which is capable of producing two to three notes with the help of a length of wood which is moved about inside the open end of the horn. The Kinnaura tribe of Himachal Pradesh have a horn instrument very similar to that of the Garos with a similar name called Haran Singha. Both the *Singga* and the Haran Singha have no holes or keys and are used for sounding blasts and are of ancient origin. The Kinnaurs are greatly influenced by Tibetan religion and culture due to their proximity to Tibet, whereas the Garos trace their origin from Tibet. The Garos have a simple way of teaching

---

9 A. Playfair, *op. cit.*, p.43.

10 Dewansing Rongmuthu, *The Folk Tales of the Garos*, Department of Publication, University of Gauhati, Guwahati, 1960, p.279.

the art of playing the trumpet. Since they have no written music, they use their own voice like, for example, *tuu ru ruu, tuu ru ruu* !

The *Sanai* is most probably an imitation of the Indian *senai.* It is made, however, out of the long gourd with a tiny bamboo piece which has a quarter of an inch hole in which a small slip or tongue is cut downwards in the upper surface of the peeled bamboo. This instrument has six stops (Plate-VI).

The other trumpet type of instrument is the Kal which is made by joining together different sized bamboos tightly, from the biggest to the smallest. It is a long trumpet somewhat like the ones used by the Tibetan monks. This is an instrument used by the *Rugas* (Plate-VII).

The familiar Jews harp is known to the Garos, and is called *Gongmina.* It is carved out of a tin slip of bamboo about 4 inches long and half in width. It is so cut that a thin tongue runs down the centre of the slip connected therewith at one extremity only. At one end a short piece of string is fastened to the Jews harp and to the other a small bamboo handle is attached. The instrument is held between the thumb and the forefinger of the left hand, placed between the teeth so that they touch it lightly, and the string is given a succession of sharp tugs by means of the handle held in the right hand to produce a twanging humming sound. Incidently, the original name of this instrument was 'Jaw's harp' but somehow it was misnamed 'Jews harp' although it has nothing to do with Jewish history of music.[11] The system of playing this instrument is given in this way:

Ra, ra, ra, ra, ra, ra,
Gong gegong ang.ke grong gegong,
Bi.lik kambe ritimchong gegong.[12]

11 Noman Lloyd, *The Golden Encyclopedia of Music,* Paul Hamlyn, London, Sydney, 1968.

12 Llewellyn R. Marak, *Ibid.*, p.3.

III. Chordophones: The Garos have two types of string instruments that I have come across and these are the *Dotrong* which is very similar to a mandolin and the *sarenda.*

The *Dotrong* is a six stringed instrument with no visible frets. It is played with the help of a plectrum made of flat bamboo or steel which is attached by a string to tiny bells. These bells are held between the fingers holding the plectrum so that a jingling sound is produced while plucking or strumming the strings. In the old days indigenous strings were used but now these are replaced by wires. The body is carved out of a solid piece of wood and is boat shaped with a long neck. Lizard skin is used to cover the junction between the main body and the neck, a tiny space is made in the main body with a hinge door to store the plectrum and bells. This instrument can be seen in West Garo Hills border areas. We see strong influence of the plains area in the instrument as well as in the manner of singing in this area (Plate-IX).

The *sarenda* is a one-stringed instrument, very much like a violin. The body is carved out of *Gambil* wood (*Careya arborica*) and the strings are made out of animal gut or the bark of the *Kilkra bol* (*Celtis orientalis*). A deep and fairly wide hollow is carved out in two parts. The lower end is covered with lizard skin (preferably) or by animal hide, and is held in place with the help of tiny wooden pegs. This serves as the sound box. The string is tied to one end (near the sound box) and on the neck side it is wound by a wooden key. It has a movable bridge called *bora*, made of the bamboo. This is played with the help of the *Bangchri* or bow made of bamboo and vegetable fibre string, preferably the fibre of the *sawe* (sago palm) (Plate-X).

IV. Membranophones: The Garos have a wide range of drums ranging from 4 ft. 3 in. in length to the tiniest which will be only about 5 in. in length. They prefer the *Gambil* wood (*Careya arborica*) for the frames of the drums. The wood is hollowed through with a sharp tool called *Batra* which is made by the *Ate Kamal* or local blacksmith. The time taken to hollow out one log for a drum which is 4 ft. 3 in. is four days. Each long drum requires two hides of the cow. The shape of the drum is larger in diameter on the left hand side and narrow on the right hand side. Once the shape of the drum is completed the hide is prepared to be strung on the open ends. Before this is done, the hair from the hide is removed with the help of water and hot ash and scrapped with a bamboo - this is known as *Kimil siksika* (scrapping of hair). Long strands of hide are required to string the hide from end to end. In order to get a knotless strand, the hide is cut in a circular system from the centre of one piece of hide, in this way they can get a rope as long as 360 feet from one hide. The knots used around the hide to give it a firm hold is known as *Chinabak.* extra hide is neatly tucked inside and this is called *Meribila.* Tuning of the drum is done by tapping the side of the hide. In this way, the strings automatically tighten. Some pebbles are put inside the drum to give it life.[13] The drums are usually hung from the neck and played by both hands while dancing, and at times, they are placed on the ground and played sitting.

The different types of drums are Dadigipa and Rikakgipa, which are slimmer and have a higher pitch than the others; Ongrimgipa which is larger and has a lower pitch; Atong or Gitchu dama; Gara Ganching; Awe and chisak dama; which is of four types; Ruga and chibok dama, these also are low pitched drums; Dama Dalsang or Kodoreng also known as Nagra; Kram which has two other smaller ones attached to it known as Kram Nadik and Bitchimani Bisa. Except for the Nagra, Kram, Nadik and Bitchimani Bisa, all the other

---

13 As told to me by Agat Sangma of village Selbalgre, West Garo Hills, 27.1.1992.

drums are kept in the Nokpante and the Bandasal or rest house (Plate XI).

The Garos have different styles of playing the drum depending on the area they come from. They also have different players such as, a single lead drummer known as *Dadigipa*, one accompanist or second drummer called *Rikkakgipa,* and any number of bass drummers known as *Onlgrimgipa.* They have a unique method of teaching the different pitches and beats to the learner through a collection of rhythmic poems. As they have no written music, this was one of the most effective ways of teaching and remembering the rhythm and beat.

The following are the drum beats in rhyme form for Wangala dance followed by the A·bengs:

1. Dadigipa (Lead Drummer - A single drummer leads)

   Tengtang dimita,
   Tengtang dimita.....

2. Chongchanggipa or Rikkanggipa (Second Drummer - Single drummer plays the seconds)

   Ritang bandang, ritang,
   Ritang bandang, ritang......

3. Ongrimgipa (Bass drummers - Played by the rest of the drummers)

   Wang kimit, wang kimit,
   Wang kimit, wang kimit.

4. Dama Dalsang (Double bass - played together with the rest)

   Wang kimit, wang kimit,
   Wang kimit, wang kimit.

   Grang kimit, grang kimit
   Grang kimit, grang kimit.

The other rhymes are:

1. *Ding dadi kimita, Nomil ja.teng rimita*
   Gong.gijako gong.ata, Changgijako changata.
2. *Chambil gongdang mesenga, Deba gnang seenga*
   Chambil rongsa godoat, Chambil rongsa kole kat.
3. *Aram mikka simdapa, jrang jrang kimita,*
   Aram mikka simidapa, jrang jrang kimita.
4. *Dadi imchang gimitchang, dingdading kimit,*
   Dadi imchang gimitchang, dingdading kimit.
5. *Grim cheng, grim*
   sare oak oaka, gokarek gook.[14]
6. *Nang·ni jikba dingtanga*
   Angni jikba dingtanga.
7. *Pante aksan dotdengdeng, dotdengdeng,*
   Pante aksan dotdengdeng, dotdengdeng.
8. *Jajong aram simdapa, jrangjrang kimita,*
   Aram mikka simdapa, jrangjrang kimita.
9. *Dentaka dentaka, nomil pante neng·taka,*
   Dentaka dentaka, nomil pante neng·taka.
10. *Winaesa chimita, winaesa chimita,*
    Winaesa chimita, winaesa chimita.
11. *Dengatang te·pattang, An·tangtangni skatang,*
    Dengatang te·pattang, an·tangtangni skatang.
12. *Panteba dingtangha, nomilba dingtangha,*
    Panteba dingtangha, nomilba dingtangha.
13. *Re·angode dubamong, nigamode rajamong,*
    Re·angode dubamong, nigamode rajamong.
14. *Samamia budola, samamia budola,*
    Samamia budola, samamia budola.
15. *Ranjeng ginjeng sammitip,*
    Ranjeng ginjeng sammitip.

---

14 Llewellyn R. Marak, *op. cit.*, p.3.

16. *Grimcheng, grimcheng..........*
(This is played during Dokmijengao Dokani or Chu ringna dokani which means before drinking).

17. *Dedegitik, dedegitik............*
(This played during *Wangalani somoeo, Chu rugalana skang, Wanti su·mitingo, Pura nia,* i.e. before the offering of the rice beer to the Gods, while pounding the rice to make rice powder. Here the *Kram* or sacred drum gives the lead).

18. *Tingtingkok tingkok, dalneo tok,*
Damdilo tok...........
(This is played during *Wanti toko doka,* i.e. during the rice powder smearing ceremony. Here the *Kram* gives the lead).

19. *Chapsni kingsni,*
Chapsni kingsni.........
(This is played during *Rugalmitingo dokani,* i.e. while offering rice beer to the Gods. Here the *Kram* gives the lead).

20. *Mikka wasi, wasi, wasi,*
Ma·su mitip, mitip, mitip........
(This is played during *Wangalao chachat so·na skang,* i.e. before burning incense before the *wangala* ceremony. Here again the *kram* gives the lead).

21. *Miktak, miktak, miktak, miktak,*
Chu ringo, miktak, chu ringo miktak........
(This is played during *Cha·chat so·o dokani,* i.e. while burning the incense. The *kram* gives the lead again).

22. *Mangarik, mangarik, mangarik,*
Mangadin, mangadin, mangadin....
(This is the beat during *Mande siao dokani* i.e. during a funeral, and the *kram* is played).

23. *Delang kimit, kimit,*
Delang kimit, kimit.......

(This is played during *Delang so·ao dokani*, i.e. during the final funeral rite when the remains are burnt. Every one plays the drums together).

During the Wangala festival, the long drums are slung from the neck by the menfolk while they dance. While carrying the drum the dancers have to make sure that the larger side of the drum (called *Bidap*) falls on the left hand side and the narrow end (called *Bichok*) falls on the right hand side. Usually the drums are played with both hands. At times sticks are also used to beat the drum to give a different sound. This is called *Dadigol* (Drum beating with sticks). At times while the girls or the warriors dance, the men sit on the sides and play the drums.

The names of some different beats used by the *Ambengs* during the *Wangala* are:

1) *Dadia Rikkanga* (warming up)
2) *Nokkodakari Damchenga* (playing inside the house)
3) *Atila sa.ra roa* (in the courtyard)
4) *Chapekani* (to bump)
5) *Nomil chrokdilani* (beat for the maidens)
6) *Ansengani* (for enjoyment)
7) *Jawa songchi doksusani* (drum beating competition in another village)
8) *Songdal susaani* (competition between the villages)
9) *Tamasa* (a show)
10) *Spa roani* (to link up)
11) *Kambe toa* (measuring height)
12) *Pakmare ba.a* (perching like butterfly)
13) *Nomil, Pante dol dakani* (grouping of girls and boys)
14) *Nokchinapani aro Noko ringani* (entering the house and singing)
15) *Ahoia Ahoia* (Harvesting)

16) *Sara roa* (roaming in the courtyard)
17) *Jak elippani* (waving of the hand)

The different types of drum beating with sticks known as *Dadigol* are as under:

1) *Ge.ginnichi dokka* (with two sticks - the stick on the right hand is called *Bichok* and the one on the left *Bigap*)
2) *Rokom Rokom* (all kinds)
3) *An.tangni changagita* (own style)
4) *Samsa Dadigol ra.e* (with one stick).[15]

In addition to this there are 48 (forty eight) other beats used during the dance with different beats for each new step, and these are:

1) *Grong Doka* (starting drums)
2) *Gaewang Roa* (Girls' dance)
3) *Dohme Gonga* (lowering cocks' tails)
4) *Sipai Awit Roa* (warrior drum beat)
5) *Mehmang Mi Su'a* (Ghosts pounding rice)
6) *Nomil Khambe Toa* (Girls measuring height)
7) *Dama Jonga* (drum shuffling)
8) *Dama Barat Sala* (tightening drum strings)
9) *Onggal Rua* (hearth-rake demolition)
10) *Matma Siako Sogin Cha'a* (vultures feed on a buffalo's carcass)
11) *Salam Ka'a* (greeting)
12) *Gah-e Roa* (kneeling)
13) *Nomil Nipila* (girls looking behind)
14) *Jik Seka* (eloping with a lady-love)
15) *Ba'ra Su'a* (cloth washing)
16) *Chame Changa* (pursuit of lady-love)

---

15 As told to me by Agat Sangma of village Selbalgre, on 27.11.92.

17) *Chame Mikang Nia* (Lady-love's glances)
18) *Budu Rateta* (cutting a rope asunder)
19) *Chawari Sika* (capturing a bridegroom)
20) *Ba'ra Wa'gong Rama* (sunning cloth on bamboo poles)
21) *Ambretong Khola* (picking up hog-plums)
22) *Chambil Den'a* (pomelo cutting)
23) *Chu Khana* (wine offering)
24) *Mapil Roa* (bear play)
25) *Jik Sekako Rim'a* (bringing back eloped wife)
26) *Dohkru Sua* (pecking of the wild doves)
27) *Durea Rata* (cutting down cornstalks to gather corn-cobs)
28) *Oping Rata* (slashing off head-gear)
29) *Ajema Roa* (walk about)
30) *Ambretong Rua* (shaking off the Hog-Plum Fruits)
31) *Matmana Jeng On'a* (feeding fodder to a buffalo)
32) *Dama Jajoka* (realternation of drums)
33) *Rome'amaa* (girls playing elderly women)
34) *Nomil Donua* (girls playing hide and seek)
35) *Nomil Jajoka* (girls changing places changes)
36) *Nomil Ba'ra Donua* (girls hiding their cloths)
37) *Khil Oka* (picking of cotton)
38) *Nomil An'-tangni Mi-pal ko On'a* (Lady-love giving away her own share of cooked-rice)
39) *Chambil Goa* (shooting off a shaddock fruit)
40) *Nomil Dohme Suala* (girls distribute cocks' tail plumes)
41) *Nomil Kasrang Donue Ringa* (girls smoke smoking-pipes in secret)
42) *Nomil Phante Salitinga* (girls and young men drawing up together in line)

43) *Dohsik Megaru Cha'a* (parrots feed on job's tears - Coix Lachryma jobi).

44) *Chambil Mesaa* (dance of the Pomelo fruit)

45) *Makka Abong Cha'a* (monkeys feed on maize)

46) *Khil Pua* (sowing of cotton-seeds)

47) *Chame Chakoree Kattimanga* (lovers going astray through excessive anxiety).

48) *Nomil Jajong Nidoa* (girls looking up to the moon).[16]

The *Kram* is the sacred drum used only on solemn occasions like religious and *Mangona* (funeral) ceremonies. To this is tied the two other smaller drums mentioned earlier. The *Kram* is so heavily endowed with supernatural power that no one else except the owner, that is, the *Nokma* (clan chief), dares to keep in his house. It is usual for each *Nokma* to keep a sacred drum, and ordinarily all those who do so perform the ceremony of *satsatsoa* (burning of incense) at the *Wangala* festival. Before a household first acquires the drum, the man should have a dream indicating that it is appropriate, otherwise he will die. Once acquired, however, the drum, like all aspects of nokmaship, may be inherited by the heir without any additional dreams.[17]

When these drums are first made, special sacrifices are necessary. The drum to be consecrated is laid upon plantain leaves, a fowl is slaughtered, and a little of its bloods is smeared on the drum, and some of the bird's feathers are stuck to the drum by means of the blood.

The *Nagra* is also kept only in the *nokma's* house and is also believed to host a spirit just as the *kram*. It is a large drum consisting of an earthen pot covered with skin. It is sounded in order to assemble the people to the *nokma's* house when he gives an entertainment. It is also used when a special feast is given for a visitor, for announcing a death

---

16 D.S. Rongmuthu, *op. cit.*, pp.299-304.

17 Robbins Burling, *op. cit.*, p.227.

in the village and as a warning of impending danger. In a call for a feast, the first beat invites one to the feast, the second beat informs that the feast has commenced, and the third and final beat informs all those present that the drink is over and no more serving will be done.[18] This drum is not supposed to be taken out of the owner's house at all, misfortunes being certain to overtake any one who allowed this rule to be infringed.

If the *Kram* is to be played, the owner or one of his relations must be the first to strike up, and not until then may anyone else touch it. Further, nobody except the owner or one of his relations may beat the *nagra.*[19]

The Garos also used crude Maracas made of gourd filled with gravel[20] which is called a "*Rekrek*".

These musical instruments are some of the main instruments found in the Garo Hills which are fast disappearing due to the popularity of modern instruments.

---

18 Julius L.R.Marak, *op. cit.*, p.70.

19 A. Playfair, *op. cit.*, p.43.

20 Gabriella Bertrand, *Secret Land where Women Reigns*, London Robert Hale Limited, 1958, p.48.

4

CONCLUSION

From the foregoing chapters, it is obvious that the Garos, a branch of the Tibeto-Burman branch of the Tibeto-Chinese family, were the original inhabitants of the Garo hills, which is under the state of Meghalaya today. They are basically agriculturists, and so their activities throughout the year coincided with the agricultural cycle. They follow the matrilineal system, according to which the descent is traced from the mother. As they had no written script, tradition was handed down orally from generation to generation, and kept alive in this fashion.

In the study of the traditional music of the Garos, we come to see the vast store of wealth in this field. The Garos were lovers of music and fun. Music, which had started from rudimentary beginnings, with the imitation of the sounds of nature, was adopted and improved upon imaginatively. Mans creative ability led him to use his own voice in different ways, levels and pitches, to compose a variety of tunes, and to preserve them by oral tradition in the absence of written script. They were able to relate these tunes to different occasions like - solemn, modulated chants for religious functions like the *Amua* or *Kritas*, the lively tunes of enjoyment for happy times where all join in the singing, as in the *Dimdimdimchong* of the Wangala festival, the sensuous love songs which tickle ones senses as in the *Himangai*, the subtle, inspiring song of the *Katta agana*, the heart-rending mournful tune of the *Grapmangtata* which can move to tears the hardest heart, and the sleepy lullabies to put little ones to sleep.

The Garos of old had also learnt to use the abundant supply of natural resources in innovative ways, to make musical instruments to accompany their songs. Those instruments which they had brought along during their migration, in the distant past, were preserved so well that a few still exist today. Unfortunately, poor economic conditions forced the people to sell off these priceless possessions and thereby endanger their loss. Those that they could not bring along were remembered, and the likeness of them made out of the material available in the new land, like the *Ghal* which is a reminder of the long trumpets of Tibet.

How were the Garos able to preserve all this without any written literature? one may ask. The Garos had a unique institution through which the preservation of all their art, craft and culture was assured. This was through the institution of the *Nokpante* (Bachelors' dormitory), where the young boys were imparted knowledge in all fields of life. It was in fact the life centre of the society. The villages used to resound with the sound of various instruments every evening, while the boys practised and improved their skills. In the jhum fields, you would invariably hear the soothing lilt of the flute being played by a watchman on the *Borang* or the tree house.

Unfortunately, with the conversion of the Garos into the new religion, i.e., Chrisuianity, which spoke about the putting aside of the old and taking on the new, this extremely important institute was also done away with. For in the *Nokpante* were also taught the rituals of the animistic religion. The introduction of education and the school system also had its effect. The schools gradually became the centre for the youths. The pupils lived in the house of the teacher-cum-preacher, as the *Nokpante* became unsuitable for their studies. Boarding schools thus replaced the dormitory system. As a result, the *Nokpante* system slowly but gradually deteriorated due to neglect, and with it died an important establishment of the society, the main intent of which was to guide the youths, and to preserve the indigenous art and culture of the people. The village of Emangre in south Garo hills, which boasted of having nine *Nokpantes* until recent times, has none at all now. The ruins of some of them stand witness to the neglect of an age old institute of the Garos. However, we cannot place a flat blame on Christianity. The traditional Garo society still exists today and some of the old customs and culture is still being followed by the new society such as the clan and sub-clan system. This lack of interest in their musical heritage has been brought about by the influence of modern western and Indian music, which can be seen in today's songs. Bengali influence in the border areas of West Garo hills can be seen in the musical instruments such as the *Sanai* and the decoration on the *Dotrong*, as well as in the form of singing. The more popular songs of today are adaptations of Hindi and western music. Concerted effort was not made by the elders to inculcate pride in traditional music as opposed to modern music. Innovative music was not introduced to catch the interest of the youth who needed fresh and interesting music to capture and retain their attention in the traditional tones and tunes. It is heartening to see that in this new age, it is the very religion which has been blamed for the disappearance of traditional music that is reviving interest in traditional music. Traditional musical instruments are being used to accompany gospel songs and Garo modern songs. In recent times competition are being held among the school children of Tura on traditional music and dance, to build up the interest of the children. This is a very positive step being taken by the people. In fact, it is entering the local pop culture in a big way. Perhaps this can be taken as one way of keeping alive, at the least, the life of Garo traditional music.

There is need to revive the interest in the musical and cultural legacy of the Garos for its continued existence. This can only be done by educating the children on the importance of retaining the old while taking on the new, so that one does not forget one's roots. This information can be imparted through books, especially in the vernacular language, inclusion of indigenous art and craft in the school curriculum, and through holding of exhibitions in such arts. Interest in the youth can be stimulated by establishing a music institute which gives instructions on traditional musical instruments. A training which should be given by the skilled elders from various parts of Garo hills, thus encouraging the old and enlightening the young on the importance of their indigenous art, while acquiring modern knowledge. The information imparted should be all round, right from the method of making of the instruments to the playing of the same. Where possible, musical notations of their traditional songs should be put down for posterity. Competitions in folk music and cultural dances among the different groups of the Garo tribes should also be encouraged to bring the groups closer, as well as to bring out the variety, interest and pride in their cultural heritage.

It is heartening to note that awakening in this aspect had already taken place in very recent times. Since 1976, a group of A.chick elders got together and introduced the "Hundred Drums" festival which has since been successfully celebrated every year, as a way of preserving and promoting Garo traditional songs, music, dances and games. Further, this festival provides an opportunity for groups from various villages to interact with each other. In this way, much is being done to capture the interest of the youth, as well as to showcase the culture of the Garos and preserve it for posterity.

BIBLIOGRAPHY

Alfred, Einstein, *A Short History of Music,* London Illustrated edition, 1979.

Bangshell, B.S., *Sonajing,* Tura, 1964.

Bertrand, Gabrielle, *The Secret Lands where Women Reign,* London, Robert Hale Limited, 1958.

Burling, Robbins, *Rengsanggri,* Philadelphia, 1963.

Choudhury, Bhupendranath, *Some Cultural and Linguistic Aspects of the Garos,* Lawyer's Book Stall, 1958.

Garo Literary & Cultural Society (edJourn.), *Do.kua (Kadimgimin),* Shillong, November-December 1982.

Garo Literary & Cultural Society (ed.), *Do.kua (Kadimgimin),* Shillong, January-February 1983.

Garo Literary & Cultural Society (ed.), *Do.kua (Kadimgimin),* Shillong, March-June 1983.

Garo Literary & Cultural Society (ed.), *Do.kua (Kadimgimin),* Shillong, July-October 1983.

Garo Literary & Cultural Society (ed.), *Do.kua (Kadimgimin),* Shillong, November December 1983.

Garo Literary & Cultural Society (ed.), *Do.kua (Kadimgimin),* Shillong, January-February 1984.

Garo Literary & Cultural Society (ed.), *Do.kua (Kadimgimin),* Shillong, March-April 1984.

Garo Literary & Cultural Society (ed.), *Do.kua (Kadimgimin),* Shillong, May-June 1984.

Garo Literary & Cultural Society (ed.), *Do.kua (Kadimgimin),* Shillong, July-October 1984.

Garo Literary & Cultural Society (ed.), *Do.kua (Kadimgimin),* Shillong, November-December 1984.

Garo Literary & Cultural Society (ed.), *Do.kua (Kadimgimin),* Shillong, January-February 1985.

Garo Literary & Cultural Society (ed.), *Do.kua (Kadimgimin),* Shillong, March-April 1985.

Garo Literary & Cultural Society (ed.), *Do.kua (Kadimgimin),* Shillong, May-June 1985.

Garo Literary & Cultural Society (ed.), *Do.kua (Kadimgimin),* Shillong, July-August 1985.

Garo Literary & Cultural Society (ed.), *Do.kua (Kadimgimin),* Shillong, January-February 1986.

Garo Literary & Cultural Society (ed.), *Do.kua (Kadimgimin),* Shillong, March-June 1986.

Garo Literary & Cultural Society (ed.), *Do.kua (Kadimgimin),* Shillong, July-October 1986.

Garo Literary & Cultural Society (ed.), *Do.kua (Kadimgimin),* Shillong, September-October 1995.

Garo Literary & Cultural Society (ed.), *Do.kua (Kadimgimin),* Shillong, November-December 1995.

Goswami, Roshmi, *"The Essence of folk Music with special reference to Punjabi Music"*, 1992.

Klaus, Liepman, *The Language of Music,* U.S.A. 1953.

Marak, Caroline R., *Influence of English on Garo Poetry with Particular Reference to Three Authors,* NEHU, 1985.

Marak, Harendra W., *A.chik Aganbewalrang,* NEHU, 1983.

Marak, Jobang D., *The Garo History,* Sangma Books and Prints, Tura, West Garo Hills, 1982 (2nd Edition).

Marak, Julius, *Serejing Aro Waljan,* 1988.

Mehta, R.C., *Studies in Musicology,* Bombay, Baroda.

Modern Illustrated Encyclopedia, (Vol. 14), McGraw-Hill Far Eastern Publishers (S) Ltd. - Singapore, 1972.

Playfair, A., *The Garos,* London, David Nutt, 57, 59, Long Acre, 1909.

Prajanananda, Swami, *Music of the South-Asian People* (Vol. I), Ramakrishna Vedanta Math; 19-B, Rajkrishna Street, Calcutta, 1979.

Ray, C.R., *The Music and Musical Instruments of Southern India and the Deccan,* B.R.Publishing Corporation, 461, Vivekananda Nagar, Delhi, 1977.

Rongmuthu, D.S., *Folktales of the Garos,* Dept. of Publication, University of Gauhati, 1960.

Rongmuthu, D.S., *Epic Lore of the Garos,* Dept. of Tribal Culture and Folklore Research, 1967.

Sangma, Brucellish K., "The Contribution of Garo Women to Garo Literature", *Mothers' Union Golden Jubilee Souvenir,* 1991.

Sangma, Mihir, *Maniani Bidik,* Nabajiban Press, 66 Grey, Calcutta, 1989.

Sangma, Mihir, *Pagitchamni Ku.Bisring,* Nabajiban Press, Calcutta, 1982.

Sangma, Milton S., *History and Culture of the Garos,* Books Today, Oriental Publishers, 1981.

Scholes, Percy A., *The Oxford Companion to Music,* London, Oxford University Press, 1970-'75.

Appendix –I

DANI DOKA

Oho anga dania,
Oho anga Radaa.
Anga dani dokonga,
Chinga rada ring'onga.
Ia nokding Mite,
Ia bolding Katchi.
Mite knabo,
Katchi ra'chakbo.
Mite indi rebo,
Katchi indi janibo.
Mite ka'chaongnabe,
Katchi inamingnabe.
Ia nokni depante,
Ia bolding sa'mea.
Misiko rodilnajok,
Saljongko jin'dilnajok.
Selbalni balana,
Mandalchini chong'ana.
Do'reng rochokalengjok,
Pilgim ba'rimalengjok.
Manjurini Mite,
Chusimrani Katchi.
Chusimrao pongrengo,
Roe piniknakjok,
Jan'e anganajok.
Ki'tingo mia ripok,
Jakpongo jaksil santok

DANI DOKA

oh anga radara oe anga dania Bima pe'e ni-
na haianga Saljatchie Kakuja haianga Skon taru raku-
ja haianga Ja'pa Kisil Kakuja haianga Ameko maneko
haianga Bima pe'ia gita haianga ambiko pilleko
haianga Saljatchia gita haianga

DANIA

Saksa ring'dilgen (lead singer):- Hai anga dania!

Jinma (altogether):- Hai anga!
Haianga radaa!
Hai anga!

Hai dani danggea,
rome roo rochoka,
Jakpa dareng de'toka,
Teting nongpeng nongtoka,
Hai ki'ting nongboda,
Hai jakpa de'boda.
Banan jae roknajok,
Banan tingkil ripnajok,
Gitol bisimitrara,
Dachi rengrimitrara,
Rotako chenchota,
Wa'singtokko tingtoto.
Ki'ting nongneng nongtoja,
Jakpa dareng de'toja,
Wa'singtokko tingtinge,
Chigringko ringringe,
An'chengko mande dake,
Stilko merim goe.
Pakma rikrak rikrako,
Segin ching'chet ching'cheto,
A'ni timbol groo,
chini manggi asuo,
Prem prem totoa,
ching'chet ching'chet piloa.
Pakmatangna sokbajok,
Segintangna nabajok.
Pakma rikrak rikrako,
Segin ching'chet ching'cheto,
Ripamchi ame grio
Ta'maku mikgil griko.

Appendix - II

GONDA DOKA I

Gongminaba gongchidok,
Gongsaksan dokgine;
Do'sioba magina,
Do'sa siarigine.

Do'do do'rimitgita,
Ragong bolbijakgita;
Nikrikaijok bimangko,
Salni napangagita.

Ho hogera hogera,
Ringbo na'a segera.
Nang'ni ga'batamangmang,
Songdu chigitangmangmang.

Sansareko sansea,
Nokon me'mang gnangkon;
Etaleba nijajok,
Na'a nika dongakon.

Agrangoni matchuko,
Ba'jok nang'ko mil'amna;
Nikgijaba ruutjok,
On'bo jakko salamna.

Bolo budu wedoa,
Bolna bate wejawa;
Nang'ni angko galoba,
Batakode man'jawa.

Gonda Doka: Tune II(a)

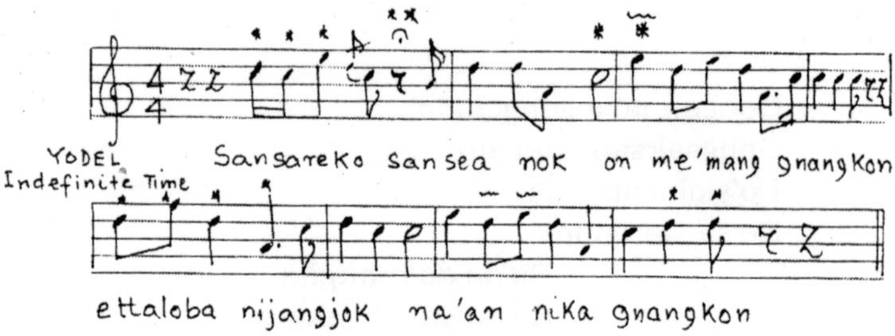

Gonda Doka: Tune II(b)

GONDA II

Mea:- Gondareko dajingjeng, pangna koe ringnade,
'Nang sariko da-mikneng, pangna sari ranade.

Mechik:- Gondamari gondanok jako tangka koledok,
Dodko an'cheng doancheng, chame angko salangcheng.

Mea:- Anti chola genjiko, ra'jok anga intale,
Boning sana mikchaa agan angna rongtale.

Mechik:- Chidareni himhime, knajajok kurangko,
Nokgil sawe bijime, nikrikjajok mikkangko.

Mea:- Milsi duri saknaode, chisakani kilkara,
Dai kode nangjawa, an'ching pante me'trara.

Mechik:- Nambatgipa mibisa, charirae geboda,
Mikkang bimang nampaja, kasaachi raboda.

Mea:- Na'banggni satnaba, na'banggni na'giri
Deko bana kenesa, nomil roa segiri.

GONDA

Appendix - III

CHERA SOLA

Aio..Jingjangmani a'songde,
Nongaljani a'jade;
Noking hajalsni banga,
Bi'sa tasisni jela unode.

Ranggol dru weramea uade,
Amak debarikramsa unode;
Songa mingsing minggama jingjangmani a'songko,
Chasong agangipasa Ruthamani chigako.

Ho.. Jingjang noa Ruthara,
Na'notanga nomila Ganggara;
Namanaan agana bisako,
Nitoanan mingsinga nomilko.

Mandean ba'jokma bisongko,
Mitean dakbisaljokma umangko;
Rim'e gipaknagitik Ruthako,
Chae ku'dimnagitik Ganggako.

Ho.. Wari jaknamgijao Ruthade,
Cham saegijao Ganggade;
Ja'an chinnik witenga anoa,
Kni gisi galenga nomila.

Morena hajalsana rama bake roenga,
Modena tasisana ritchong tinne kal'enga;
A'gil anojokona Ruthara,
Jengsa nomiljokona Ganggara.

Aio.. Sa'ra kinte bneka bnekja mesana,
Nokra wa'se di'ipa di'ipja chrokna;
Minni ama Susimemani siao gita,
Meja Sansareani salo namsanga gita.

Chera Sola

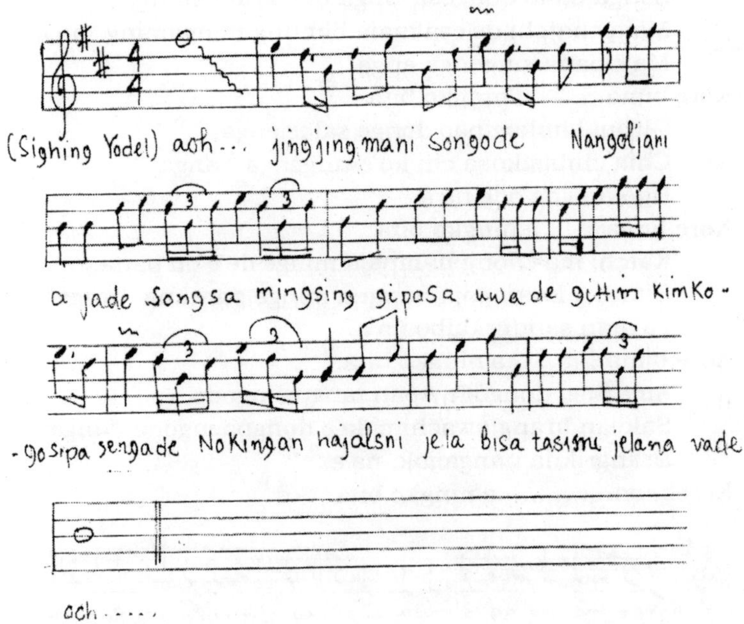
(Sighing Yodel) aoh... jingjing mani Songode Nangoljani
a jade Songsa mingsing gipasa uwa de gittim kimko-
-gosipa sengade Nokingan hajalsni jela Bisa tasisni jelana vade
ach....

Appendix - IV

KORE BIMA

Kore bima redingko mala,
Asilika a'ningko bita,
Kore bima redingko mala,
Asilika a'ningko bita.
    Songa bano dongesa chiga bako ringaming,
    Maia chatchi de'esa maia bimung mingaming "na'a,"
    Ma'sipana singenga anga.
Kore bima.........a'ningko bita.
    Gittim kimkogipao donge salasienga,
    Chia chibisikosa chi ko'e ringenga " anga"
    Uijokma da'ode na'a.
Kore bima ....a'ningko bita.
    Katchi ma'chong nampaja minge de'e on'pana,
    Bimung knatopaja nangna minge parakna "anga"
    Ja'man sandirikaibo na'a.
Kore bima............a'ningko bita.
    Ama sagi dongode Apan tangpaengode,
    Saksan brangjawachim da'o dongpaengode "anga"
    Brangrikna nangaijok, na'a.
Korebima.............a'ningko bita.

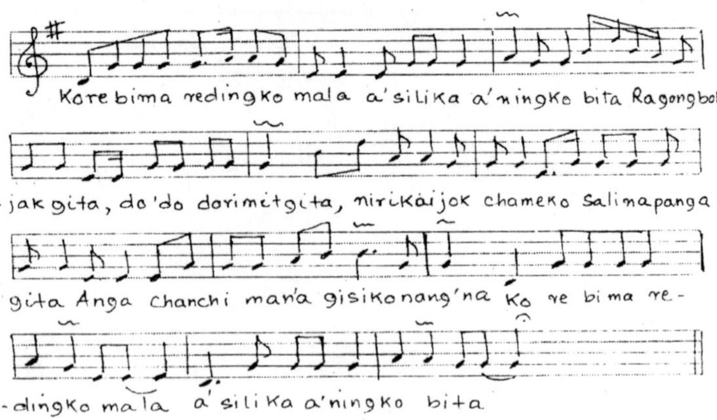

Appendix - V

AROWAKA

Bibal rimit balenga.......Aowaka,
A'sarini besual...........Arowaka.
Songgipino dongoba........Arowaka,
Gisikode da gual..........Arowaka.

A'ba bolrichonggita.......Arowaka,
Do'ka manggisimgita.......Arowaka.
Mangrorenge namachim......Arowaka,
Indioba sakgisim..........Arowaka.

Bolgisiman bolgisim.......Arowaka,
De'o rongjirikala.........Arowaka.
Sakgisiman sakgisim.......Arowaka,
Tariode namkala...........Arowaka.

Bolo wegagipade...........Arowaka,
Budu jaksimagita..........Arowaka.
Na'song asongakode........Arowaka,
Nika jiksesagita..........Arowaka.

A'ba baring nagako........Arowaka,
Song'e cha'e namkala......Arowaka.
Ke'a nanga ongjasa........Arowaka,
Na'a man'na boonga........Arowaka.

Appendix - VI

RERE RING'A

Ha-re-re, ha-re-re ...
Chi ruru mikoa chi ruru mikoa,
Chio ripa songchoke chio ripa songchoke
Hunumande ma'giri atchijok badike,

Ha-re-re, ha-re-re ...
Matmani gitoko matmani gitoko,
Pataetjokde kolongrong pataetjokde kolongrong,
Na'a mande alsia nape tua ro'rong,

Ha-re-re, ha-re-re ...
Nangko sati wingana nangko sati wingana
Nokma ine donginok nokma ine donginok
Nokcha sokangjakode anggitaan dilpanok,

Ha-re-re, ha-re-re ...
Sala salniangengjok sala salniangengjok,
Na'a miko song'jama na'a miko song'jama,
Kam ka'e okrijok na'a mi on'jama,

Ha-re-re, Ha-re-re ...
Balpakrani a'brio Balpakramni a'brio
Do'de bipa mesara do'de bipa mesara,
Song chel'achi renaba anga nang'nan ka'sara,

Ha-re-re, Ha-re-re...

Rere Ring.a: Tune (a)

Accl.: accelerando – at a fast pace.

Rere Ring.a: Tune (b)

Appendix - VII

DORO RING'A

Ho-ho-A'ningchi drengchengbaa,
Chiningchi wanbolchengbaa-mo
Ma'gipani a'songo
Biambini chigao,
An'chengko mande dake
Kasiko do'me pote,
Duaringko ringringa-mo,
Wasingtoko tingtoka,
Ku'chisa imbingbingbame.
Ho-Ho-Chratanga Asia
Depantea Maljara,
Pong sualo dongpaja
Mi rarono cha'paja.
Ku'sik ku'an aganja,
Misina mikchikimja,
Saljongna jakpa on'ja,
Roo ino romongja,
Donga ino dongchapja.
Ina marang nange,
Starang gaesa-mo,
Asiko matcha chikjok,
Maljako buga ra'jok.
Smupako gimaa,
Renggolpake salnia,
Dimchang okikio,
Wari ja'skuo.

Appendix - VIII

BOEL RING'A

Salaramni Saliramna bilenggipa do'ma,
Angni ka'samanchenggipa uiama sawa.
    Mikka wana chobaenga aram dandak dandak,
    Ka'satangko chanchiaton gisik bildik bildik.
Giting bilni salakimo chadengengagita,
Chanchimana gisiktango dongrimengagita.
    Mikchitangko kali sim'e jaksiko pen dake,
    Seatenga anga nang'na gisiko dukan gape.
Simdik sindik chobaenggipa salgisakni aram,
Angni nang'na seatako donabene ramram.
    Dal'begipa Rajan' killa pe'nade amjawa,
    Angni nang'na ka'saako gualna manjawa.
Chel'kalao niatode a'brian bo'rot borot,
Ka'satangna chanchiaton mikchian ringrot ringrot.
    Namnamgipa nitogipa bibalrang dongoba,
    Chu'ongkuja tosusana nang'kode indiba.
Dal'a dalbregija na'a nama te'rakbalbal,
Wagam kitma bitchri aro ku'chil mandal bibal.
    Nang mikkang bimang nama chanchinan amsokja,
    Mandeanma mitesama uina ampilja.

BOEL

Key: C.

Nito - gine pul banano bal - enggipa pulrang
Citchak rimit ni-to - ri ri madim - enggiperang
Chala - ode mangen gita nika hangko rimha
Ra ngode bilé kata kene eng je - gringna

Appendix - IX

HARARA HARARA

Bol gongding gongdangko sol'ja anga naggiri,
Mamatangni rimjaode re'ja anga chawari-Harara harara.

Wa'naruni kambeo do'maski manggni,
Ia songni pantede namnambea sakgni-Harara harara.

Chiringoni ro'ongko pil'leng pil'leng gamana,
Angni mikchagipako pil'e pil'e nimana-Harara harara.

Dura mikka tel'ipa wanakama wajama,
Angni mikchagipako man'nakama man'jawa-Harara

A'dingoni me'ako ranggol pe'e cha'angjok,
Angni mikchagipako jawa seke katangjok-Harara harara.

Appendix - X

GOGAI-WAI GOSAI-WAI

Me'asa - A'wejoljol bawilna,
Chame anga Goera,
Gando makkal badingna,
Songgabate re'bara.

Ringtai'taiani (chorous) :-
Gogai-wai gosai-wai
Direng-wai —2

Me'chik - Nokman' wangalanasa,
Re'baming cha'pana,
Siru a'palanasa,
Bilbaming goserong.

Me'asa - Do'sik baoni bilbara,
Bolong agatchioni,
Nomil baoni re'bara,
Waribokgirioni.

Me'chik - Baoni pante ajara,
Nomil basena mangmang,
Baoni do'sik gakera,
Medong ratchira mangmang.

Me'asa - Ku'rang knasingsanga,
Bimang nina nitoa,
Kirang goriribao,
Bimang salo rambao.

Me'chik - Ku'rang gaantisajok,
Ku'rangkoan jejajok,
Bimang ranggoresajok,
Tochi jo'olasajok.

GOSAI

A'songmao bolboko
Silmea deangchengbajok
Chigara chengchen gipoko
Silmea jokon manbaana - aiao.

A.bakon bakkakuja
Chikon chisa rongkuja
Kumongnangrime songsul
Noksulan dongkuja - aiao.

Unomiting somoio
Waljansingba atchijok
Uni bilsi daode
Bilsi chichet ong'para - aiao.

Songdu chikarepiti
Matma maankipiti
Ate silmangariko
Doke jakalengpiti - aiao.

Amakmaba gengdangdang
Mia sualengpiti,
Dokamaba jachrangchrang
Bijak sromengpiti -aiao.

Moari makan daan daanba
Kusik aganana
A'ba jamang aona
kumong Agangrikana - aiao.

Unomitingo akal dipilokmiting
Pilak chatchirangan channe on'miting -aiao.

Kerama wakna chilmiting
Akal dobitokmiting
Pilak chatchi nangana
Channe on'miting.

Noko mako donako
Maram minga kotchude
Chuara miadongjaode
Ma'nok chanja skangde - aiao.

Appendix - XI

HIM-ANGAI

Do'rimitko nikoba, bibal rimit baloba,
Na'a angni sambao, apsan nikpaosaming
Inmana, Him.....angai !
    Da'a salde antin' sal, anti dokra kenajok,
    Bi'sa nag'ko niksoe, dingding ka'dimsognok,
    Inmana, Him....angai!
Sa'ra waltim so'ao, katta mitapengpango,
Nang'ni mola so'ako, ringe roatosaming,
Inmana, Him.....angai!
    Ta'torako me'diko, rite on'bo bi'sana,
    Anga re'angpilgnok, dongkamjawa pangnaba
    Inmana, Him....angai!
Do'rimitko nikoba, bibalrimit baloba,
Mikchatangko nikoa, ka'saman'a inoba,
Inmana, Hin.....angai!
    Jana tangka man'ako, attam soko noktango,
    Jaktang nang'na on'osa kusi ong'batgnichim,
    Inmana, Him....angai!
Deko jakkandilako, nang'ni su'a song'ako,
Nikatenga gisiko, dontongbojok na'ara,
Inmana, Him.....angai!
    Salko janggiltikpile, a'bakuko gamako,
    Do'cheluko ja'rike, nang'ni re'bapilako
    Nikata, Him....angai!
Wa'tok dikrong daksobo,tange name sokango,
Gisik ra'e Burmako,Ringepana noktango,
Basakon, Him.....angai!

Appendix - XII

NANGORERE

Ring'taitaiani:- Nangorere goserong (3)
Oe nanggo goserong.

A'baoni a'likko maina minchichottata,
Angni mikchagipako maina mikchiongata.
Wa'naruni kambeo do'maski manggni,
Angni mikchagipade namnambe sakgni.

Kera matchi tejangjang, Mangot wate bawiljang,
Baoni songni nomilming, maia chatchi de'aming.
Chiringoni ro'ongko, pileng pileng ga'mana,
Angni mikchagipako, pile pile nimana.

Ramasamni suedil, bolna bate wejawa,
Nina nitobeoba, angni jora ongjawa.
Dura mikka dilipa, wanakama wajawa,
Angni mikchagipako manakama manjawa.

A'baoni me'ako, ranggol pe'e chaangjok,
Angni mikchagipako, jawa seke katangjok.
Nono gisimgipade, Ramasamni demechik,
Nomil silbegipara, na'a sani demechik.

Appendix - XIII

SONATCHI

Angko soinabali,
Baba angko dontaiaha
Daning Sonatchide.
Songa Patalgiri songni
Jarong nokman bisa,
Rona namma niwatesa
Chiring saporesa.
Chibima jokangenga
Songni samba joljol,
Niwate rona nama
Chiring Sappu joljol.
Gisik katong kasinate
Balwaan balsri balsri.
Indaka kusinsalko
Anga gimaatjok,
Malsin Chandra gose angko
Sambisiko on'e.
Sal gitamna gose angko
Aningo opjokde,
Baba angna ka'saenba
Gose dangalota te'sa.
Gopchakata gose danang
Angna ka'saesa.
Dangalota te'sanasa
Daketrangde angko,
Mangbilasa mikbokenming
Danang bisongde.
Indaka dukrangkosa
Gose chakna nangjok,
A'bri mendu burung jatchi
Birangnasa nangjok.
Dakketrangni mangbilosa
Angade tangchabae,
Birangnasa nangjok
Gose angadene.
Siaoni tangchaesa
Anga brangbaenba,
Goalpara songjinmao
Anga napakenga.

Appendix - XIV

OHOMA (Ambeng)

Regitchini soksola
chame jakjippagita
O...homa

Nokjangchio bawile chima
Chame jadin baarok
O...homa.

Gimbil nokma Baliram
Bala balchonangengjok
O...homa.

Na'a mao masaming
Ma'chong aganangkuming
O...homa.

Gaantini rengrenga
jojong grappagita
O...homa.

Tusio jumang nikuna
Samsenggitchue
O...homa.

Salni ama saliram
sala chokonangengjok.
O...homa.

Bolni majing kaaming
Ake goonangkuming
O...homa.

Tune II: Chisak and A.we

Version A.

Version B.

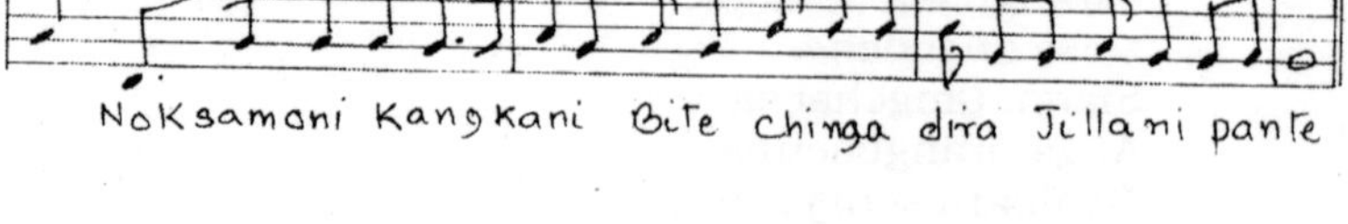

Appendix - XV

AJEA

Asiki rongbirong nabajok
Dango saljong mikchirong sokbajok
Nomila danang
Dongijako dorengreng
Aganama nomila - ha.

Madosa chasaa, etingkong kongha
Banidepante oktongtongha - o..hm
Nangni dengu dakani bite
Hatoatni babuni tupi
Nomila ha - o..hm

Na.a mao masaming
Ma'chong aganangkuming nomilaha
Bolni jasing ka.saming
Akkedonangkoaming
Nomila ha - o..hm.

Chiganggare taraka
mikkachisa waana
Watere jadila rarana
Mimacheksi ongrima aha
Ama aganatonga angade jigaljigal aha - o..hm

Appendix - XVI

BISA MU MUA

Oe-o, oe-o, oe-o
Ranggirani takraka,
Awa angjong teraka.
Chambil gongdang mesenga,
Deba gnang seenga.

Angjong ba'e mangnenga,
Bolgong gae ringrenga.
Angjong ba'ang doktepang,
Bolko kang rikkengkang.

A'o gadimdimode,
Chonggi bisi binawa.
Chio gachokchokode,
Ronggin dareng matnawa.

Masi angko kenawa,
Te'matchio ganawa.
Oe angjong gipoke,
Nabarani kimboke.

Appendix - XVII

DIMDIMDIMCHONG

Ringtaiani:-
Dimdimdimchong dadichong
Dama dokato
Nomil pante me'trarang
An'ching wangalo
Dama bangsi sikana
An'ching mesana.

1. Kotip gital ra'ako kae nipana
Bilsin gisep changsasan, an'senge nina.

2. Matchu chara milako jengogatako
Cha'e mesae an'sengna, an'ching wangalo.

3. Bilsi kari sokpingo wachi ra'gato
Mia misi akmano, an'ching wangalo.

Appendix - XVIII

ATTONG KATA

1. Ka Bandi Goera
Silang pattal janera,
Bako dakgijagipa,
Maiko man'gijagipa.
2. Ho —-
Song mongsonggipani Bandi
Gittim kimkogipani Dikki,
Nogipako Giting minga,
Manitangko So're gata.
3 Dikka nabaksni kaako,
Sika jentisni sikako,
Song'a bilsisni song'ana,
Donna karisni donna.
4. Jang'ki achakgita dal'gipa,
Timang do'bimagita pil'gipa,
Seti so'o kampiljok uade,
Bitchi chin'o man'jokna ukode.
5. Bilsisni chasongni bi'sade,
Cha'amsni gatdoe niode,
Ki'tik bon'e nikuja ina,
Nabak rim'nan sokmankuja uade.
6. Silbebejok siade Gitingba,
Nambebejok namade So'reba,
Kni rasin baksalja baksalja,
Wagam kitma bitchrija bitchrija.
7. Okstean na'bare bista,
Kni tom'o nikmana slongga,
Ku'agano ku'dambok daka,
Jaksietto jaktingot nika.
8. Nikmano niktainagitik,
Grongoba grontainagitik,
Peteng sale agano salba nangchakagita,
Ku'a knatoriri gaanti ringringagita.
9. Daka nanggo Gitinga rania,
Bebe da'nang So'rea nimila,
Bimang mangrorengreng niktainagitik,
Chet. Stuatako jakpa rachaknagitik.

Attong Kata

Note: *Ad Lib - at your own pace, freely.*

Appendix – XIX

TANTANNI SUL

Appendix – XX

HOWA SUL

Appendix – XXI

SEREJING (Tune I)

Doh is D.

Appendix – XXII

SEREJING (Tune II)

<u>Doh is E</u>.

Appendix – XXIII

SEREJING (Tune III)

Doh is E.

Appendix – XXIV

SEREJING (Tune IV)

Doh is E.

Appendix – XXV

SEREJING (Tune V)

Doh is E.

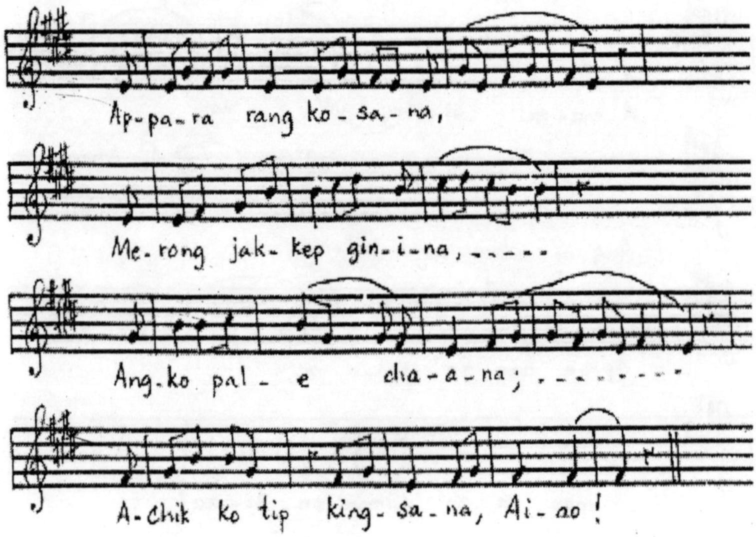

Appendix – XXVI

SEREJING (Tune VI)

Doh is E.

Plate – I: Idiophones

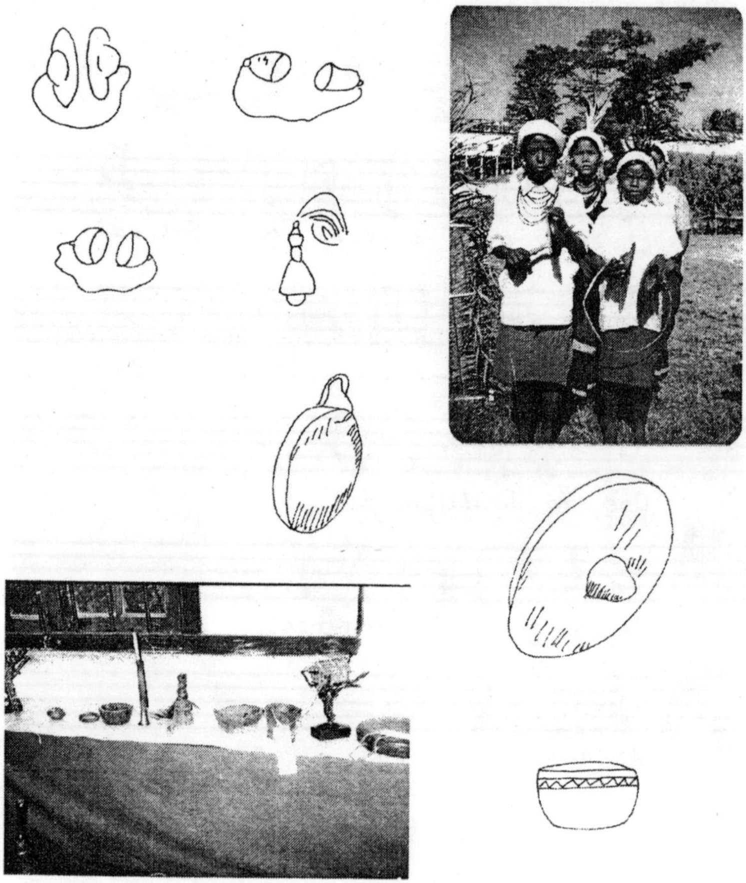

Plate – II: Idiophones – continued

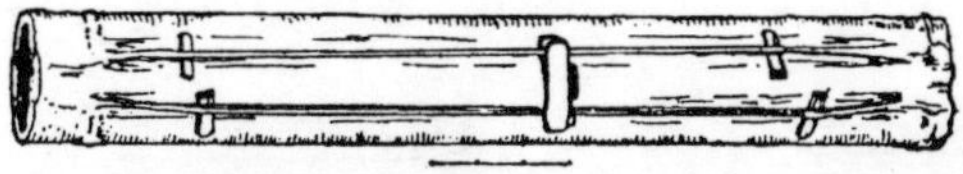

Chigring

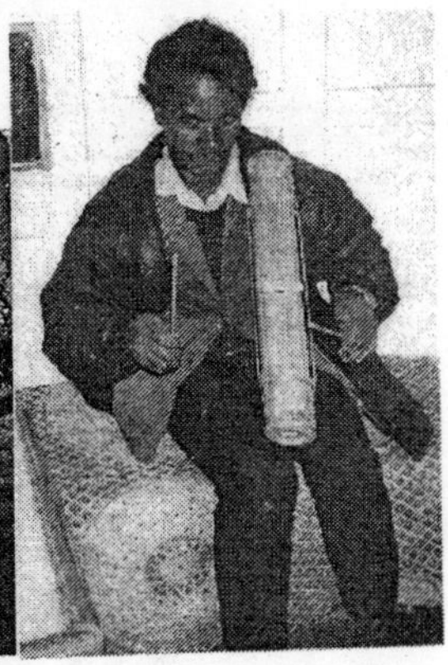

Plate – III

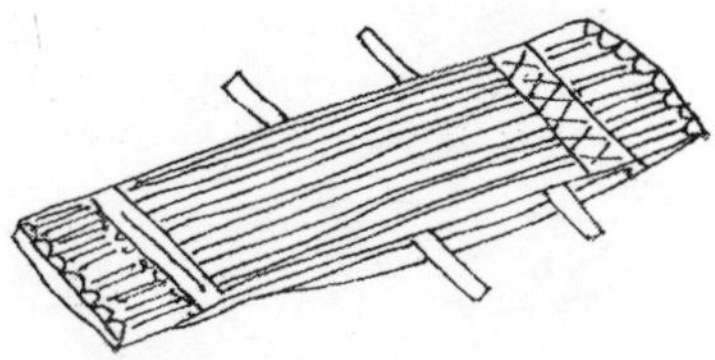

Dimchrang or Kimjim

PLATE – IV: Aerophones

A.chikrangni Sika Mòanirang (Garo Wind Instruments)

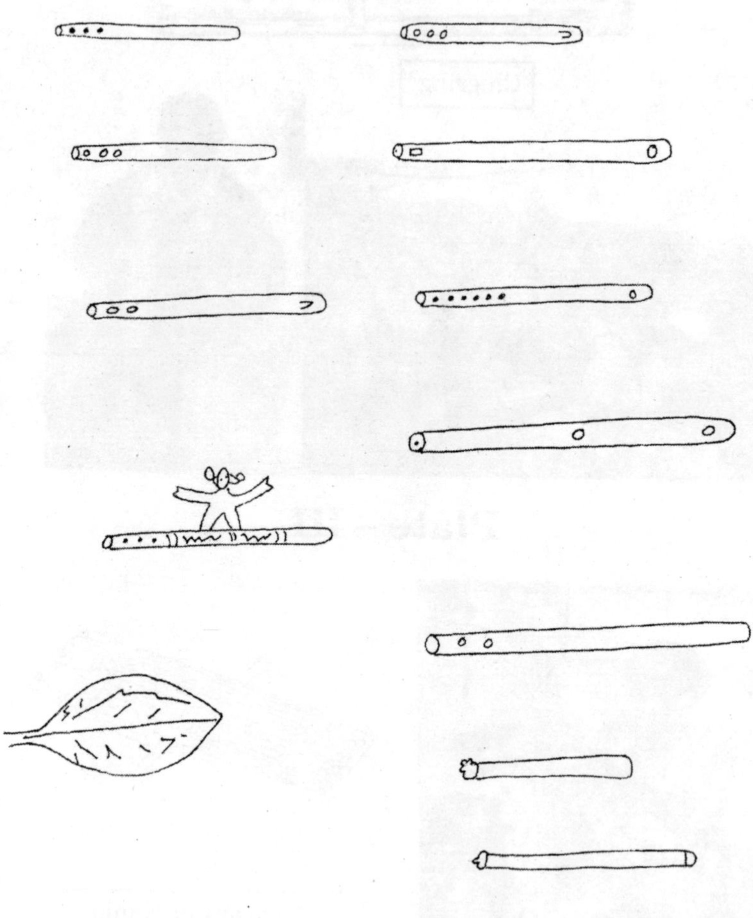

PLATE – V: Aerophones

A.chikrangni Sika Moanirang (Garo Wind Instruments)

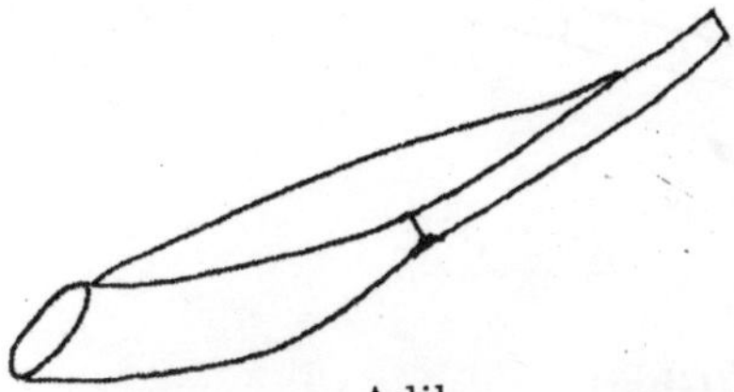

Adil

Singga

PLATE – VI

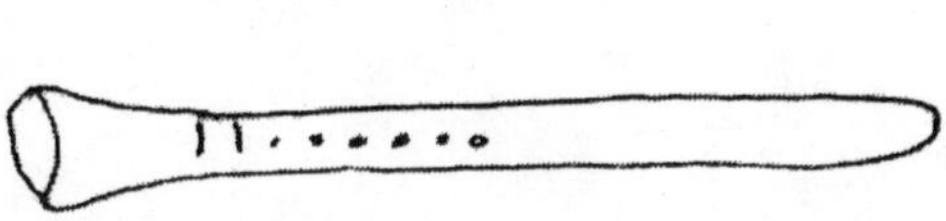

Sanai (Senai)

PLATE – VII

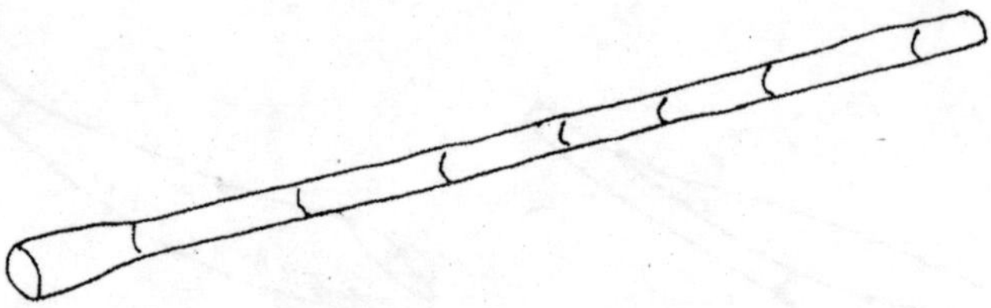

Kal (Ghal)

PLATE – VIII

Gongmina or Gonggna

Plate – IX: Chordophones

(Garo String Instruments)

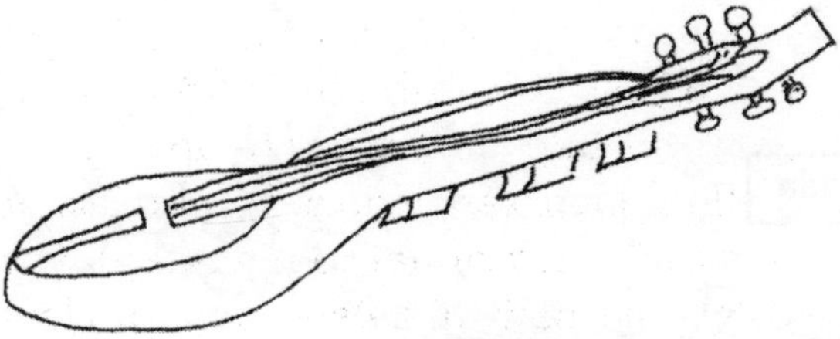

Dotrong

Dotrong

Plate – X: Chordophones – continued.

(Garo String Instruments)

Sarenda

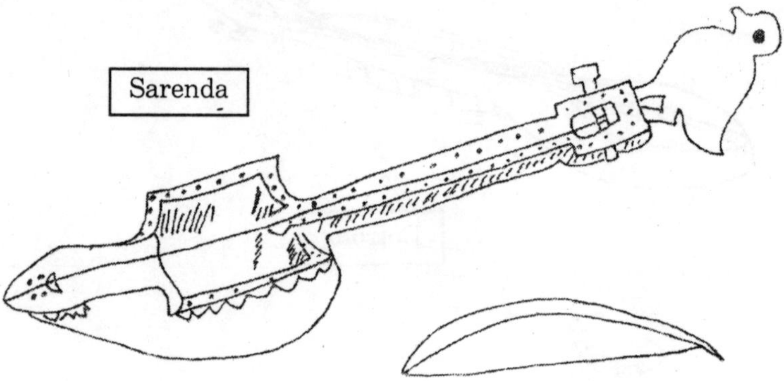

Bangchri

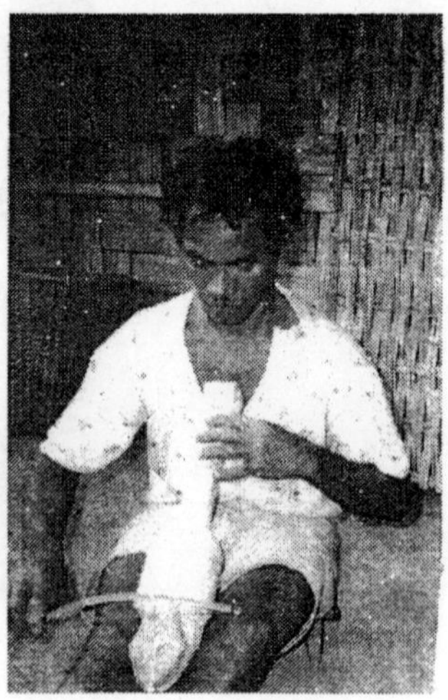

PLATE – XI: Membranophones

A.chik Dama (Garo Drums)

1. Ambeng dama:

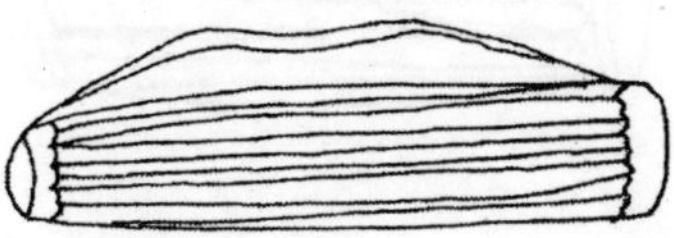

Dadigipam

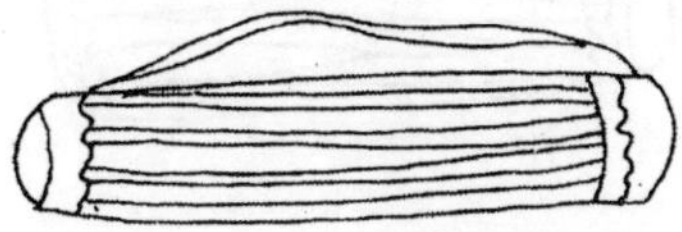

Rikakgipa

Ongrimgipa

2. A.we and Chisak dama:

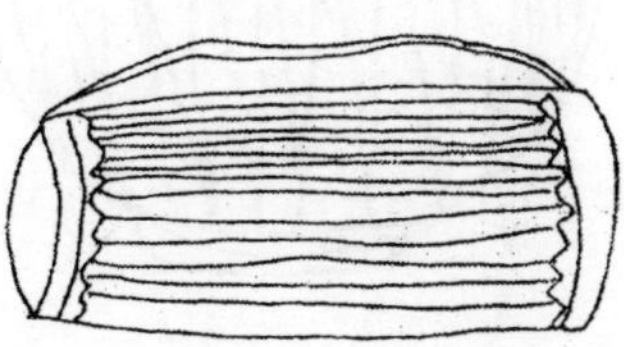

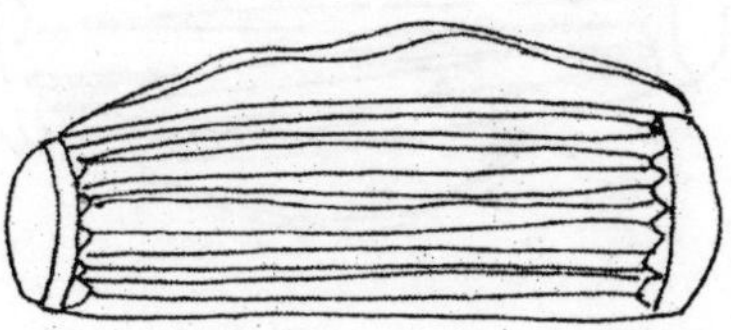

3. Attong ba gitchu dama:

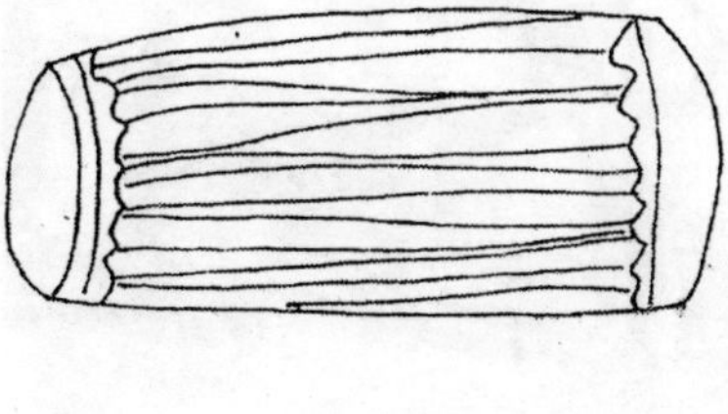

4. Gara gan.ching:

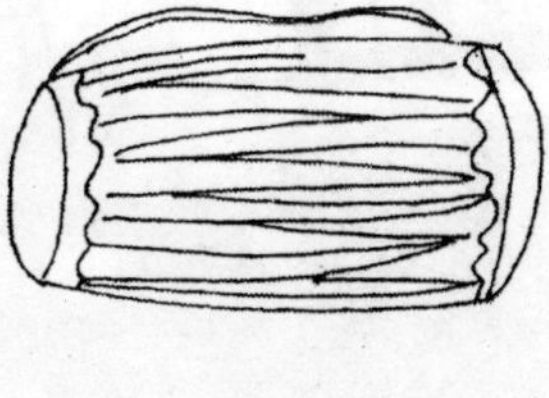

A.chik Dama (Garo Drums) – continued

5. Ruga and chibok dama:

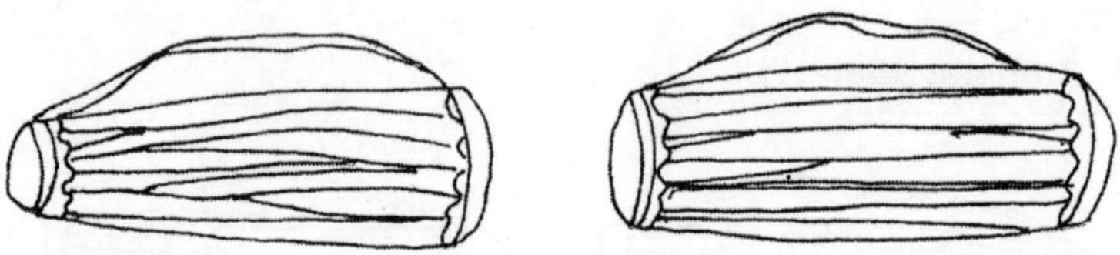

6. Kram:

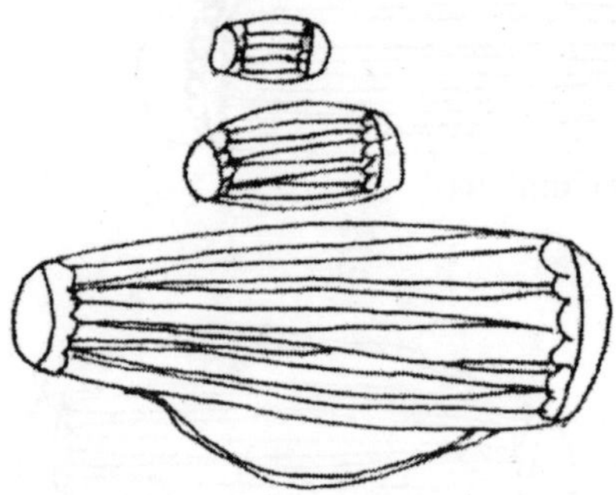

7. Nagra, Dama dalsang, Kodoreng:

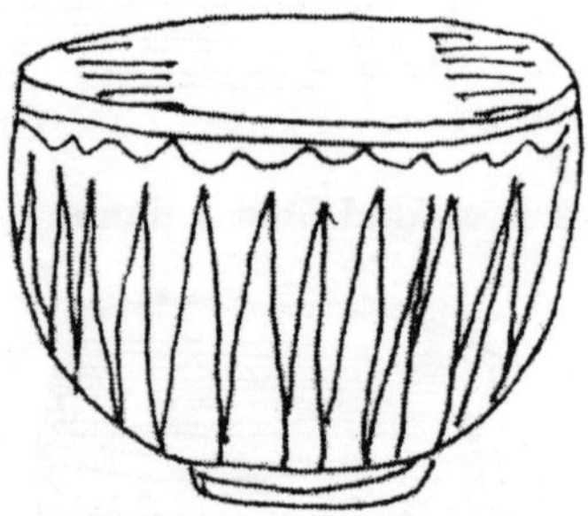

INDEX

□□□